Find & Follow

Reduce Supervisor Burnout & Improve Employee Performance by Transferring Knowledge Faster

Greg DeVore and Jonathan DeVore

© Copyright 2023 Greg DeVore II & Jonathan DeVore

All rights reserved.

No part of this publication may be reproduced, distributed, or transmitted in any form or by any means, including photocopying, recording, or other electronic or mechanical methods, without the prior written permission of the publisher, except in the case of brief quotations embodied in critical reviews and certain other noncommercial uses permitted by copyright law. Requests for permission should be directed to book@screensteps.com.

This book may be purchased for educational or business use. For more information visit amazon.com or www.screensteps.com/find-follow-book.

ISBN: 979-8-89109-183-2 - paperback

ISBN: 979-8-89109-184-9 - ebook

Contents

Online Resources vi
Introduction vii

Part I: Solving the Knowledge Transfer Problem

    Chapter 1: Defining the Pain 1
    Chapter 2: You Have Already Experienced Find & Follow . . . 15

Part II: Knowledge Operations

    Chapter 3: Measuring Where You Are At—The Knowledge Ops Maturity Model 23
    Chapter 4: The Benefits of Moving Up the Knowledge Ops Maturity Model 41

Part III: The Find & Follow Framework

    Chapter 5: Three Core Beliefs of the Find & Follow Framework 59
    Chapter 6: The Four Systems 67
    Chapter 7: What You Need for Find & Follow 77
    Chapter 8: How Will Find & Follow Be Different Than What You Are Doing Now? 81

PART IV: Implementing the Find & Follow Framework in Your Business

    Chapter 9: Build Your Knowledge Ops Team 91
    Chapter 10: The Prepare System Part 1 – Align + Define . . . 97
    Chapter 11: The Prepare System Part 2 – Design + Refine . . 111
    Chapter 12: The Train System 137
    Chapter 13: The Empower System 151
    Chapter 14: The Adapt System 157

Part V: Applying Find & Follow to Real Problems

    Chapter 15: Decreasing the Load on Tier 2 Reps 163

    Chapter 16: Scaling Your Contact Center 167

    Chapter 17: Starting a New Contact Center or Bringing on a BPO Partner. 177

    Chapter 18: Losing Key Employees. 183

    Chapter 19: Saving a Failing Contact Center. 187

PART VI: Tips for Launching Find & Follow

    Chapter 20: Choosing Where to Start 191

    Chapter 21: Addressing the Fears 197

    Chapter 22: Doing an 80% Launch 203

    Chapter 23: Optimizing Your Knowledge Operations After Launching Find & Follow .207

Part VII: Summing Up

    Chapter 24: Confidence, Consistency, and Independence. . .215

Appendix: Best Practices and Tips

    Knowledge Champions and Knowledge Ops Managers 221

    Running the Find & Follow Workshop 227

    Building Digital Guides That Can Stand Alone. 231

    5 Principles for Preparing Digital Courses 241

    Preparing Practice Activities 245

    Running Training Sessions 247

    Dealing With Challenges and Objections 255

    Creating Clarity When Procedures Seem Complicated . . .263

    Choosing a Knowledge Base or Knowledge Ops Platform . .267

    The Short Version of Everything 271

Additional Online Resources and Training 274

Acknowledgments 275

About the Authors 279

About ScreenSteps 281

Online Resources

To help you get the most out of this book, we have prepared a FREE downloadable workbook.

You can download the workbook at: www.screensteps.com/find-follow-book/workbook

If you prefer to learn in a course format, you can access accompanying courses at: www.screensteps.com/find-follow-book/courses

Additional resources are available at: www.screensteps.com/find-follow-book/resources

Introduction

Back in the early 2000s, I had just graduated from the Berklee College of Music with a degree in Composition and Film Scoring. As a recent grad, I was fortunate to get steady work with several film composers in Los Angeles. But it wasn't my degree that got me my first jobs. It was my knowledge of a software application called Logic Audio.

Apple had just purchased Logic, and because so many composers were already using Apple hardware, Logic quickly became the music software of choice. The only problem was that nobody knew how to use it.

Logic was incredibly powerful but very unintuitive. The user manual was about six inches thick and written more for the left-brain engineer than the right-brain composer. Moreover, the company was from Germany, and every couple of pages, you would come across phrases that hadn't even been translated from German into English.

My unique skill was that I was one of the few people willing to read the user manual and translate it into instructions that composers could actually use. At the time, I realized that what Logic was providing its customers was an encyclopedia when what they wanted was a recipe book.

A composer didn't want to know all the inner workings of Logic. They wanted to know how to create a 16th note arpeggio over 8 bars or how to loop a 4-bar drum groove. My job was to listen to what they wanted to do, figure out how to do it, and then teach them the recipe.

When my brother and I eventually started building documentation software, we started from the same philosophy—we would help people create documentation that looked more like recipes than encyclopedias.

Eventually, the software product we created, ScreenSteps, grew into a full-blown knowledge base platform and eventually into a knowledge ops platform (this book will explain what a knowledge ops platform is later on). While it allowed users to create all types of documents, it was especially good at creating step-by-step guides with screenshots.

Though we provided a great software tool for creating how-to guides, we didn't have a formal process for helping our customers truly transform their operations. We had some tips and ideas, but they didn't add up to a recipe that would guarantee success for our customers.

Around 2015, our company was struggling. We had developed great tools for making it really easy for customers to create knowledge bases. But we realized that in many cases, we were just providing better ways for companies to make their own version of the Logic user manual. And if there was anyone that knew firsthand that most people don't read user manuals, it was me.

Business owners and directors we spoke to didn't necessarily want a knowledge base.

They wanted employees who learned their jobs faster.

They wanted employees who could work more independently and not make so many mistakes.

They wanted employees who asked fewer questions.

And they wanted employees who could quickly adapt to change.

A Logic-like user manual wasn't going to accomplish any of that.

Around the same time, we were working with a customer named Stephanie, who worked at a BPO (a Business Process Outsourcer—a company that can take over certain business processes such as customer support calls). But Stephanie's company was in danger of losing a key client. The problem was that the client's information was so vast and complex that the BPO was struggling to hire, train, and retain enough people to fulfill the contract. New hires couldn't hit target metrics, and many employees would quit because the job was just too hard.

Stephanie knew that if she didn't solve this problem, then her company would be at risk of losing this client.

The results Stephanie achieved with our product, ScreenSteps, were jaw-dropping.

Previously, it took 60 days for a new agent to complete training and be qualified to start taking calls. With Stephanie's changes, agents started taking calls in 15 days instead of 60.

And not only were new agents trained faster, they were happier. Prior to Stephanie's changes, the BPO struggled to staff the project. Nobody wanted to work on it because it was so complex. But after her changes, it became the project everyone wanted to work on because the information was so clear.

When we saw those results, we knew we had to understand better what Stephanie was doing and how we could help other clients achieve similar outcomes. We knew that buying a knowledge base was not very exciting. But cutting time to proficiency for a new employee by 75% can be transformative for a business.

I have the blessing of working with two of my brothers, Trevor and Jonathan. Trevor has always been the developer, and Jonathan has been a jack of many trades. He is an outgoing extrovert and amateur magician with an accounting degree. Jonathan worked for several years at PwC in a role that did not fit his personality at all. It wasn't too hard for us to convince him to dump corporate America and come to work for us.

Jonathan was tasked with understanding what Stephanie had done, and what he found was that Stephanie was using our software in ways we had not ever intended. So Jonathan would report back to Trevor, and Trevor would adapt our software to better support what Stephanie was trying to do.

It Wasn't Just About Software

Based on Jonathan's research, we made many changes to our product, but we found that product changes weren't enough. People would use the new features, but the results they would get would vary wildly. Some saw dramatic improvements in training time, and some saw no improvement at all.

It was clear that technology alone couldn't drive the outcomes we wanted our customers to achieve. We needed a framework (or recipe) that our customers could use with the software to guarantee a positive outcome.

Forming the Framework

The three of us would meet every few days to review the progress with each customer, identify the roadblocks, and try to pull out the universal principles. We ran into many dead ends, but after months and months of experimentation, different parts began to fall into place.

Eventually, we settled on a framework that worked for a few customers and then a few more. Soon we saw that everyone who applied this framework saw a massive improvement in their operations.

This wasn't just dropping training time by 10% or boosting productivity by 5%. We were seeing training times drop by up to 85% and productivity increase by two or even three times.

This framework is called Find & Follow. It is a recipe for transferring knowledge to your employees faster and creating a massive impact on your operations, profitability, and culture.

That is the purpose of this book—to provide you with the concepts, frameworks, and recipes that will help you solve the training and operational challenges that have plagued your business for so long.

Some Housekeeping

While this book is primarily written from Greg's voice, it really is a collaboration between Greg and Jonathan. This was a joint effort as we worked to clarify the principles and techniques that embody Find & Follow.

We share many customer examples in the book. In each case, we have changed the names of the people involved.

We hope you find the thoughts shared here useful, the examples inspiring, and the instruction clarifying. Good luck as you begin your transformation into a Find & Follow Organization.

How to Use This Book

This may seem strange to say, but you probably don't need to read every chapter of this book. Depending on your role in your organization, you will find certain chapters more pertinent than others. Here are some suggestions on where to focus your attention.

If you are a **business owner, CEO, VP,** or **director** and just want to know if the Find & Follow is worth your attention, read Parts I, II, and III. If you want to see a list of case studies, then review Part V.

If, after all that, you want your operations, training, or quality teams to start implementing Find & Follow, have them read Parts III, IV, V, and VI.

If you are a **supervisor, manager, trainer, technical writer,** or **QA specialist** and want to evaluate the Find & Follow Framework, read Parts II and III. Then if you decide to implement Find & Follow, go on to Parts IV, V, and VI.

Obviously, if you would like to read all the sections, you are welcome to.

If none of those hats fit you, then just start at the beginning and go as far as you like. Thank you for spending some time exploring these ideas!

Part I:

Solving the Knowledge Transfer Problem

"If you can't solve a problem, it's because you're playing by the rules."
– Paul Arden, Marketer and Author

Chapter 1:

Defining the Pain

Hanging by a Thread

When Kim hopped on the Zoom call, Jonathan could tell that she was hopeful. But he could also sense that she had some doubts. That isn't uncommon. Every customer we begin working with has a mixture of excitement and fear: Excitement that we might actually be able to help them and fear that the project might turn out like most other projects they initiate in their business—a failed effort.

When Jonathan asked Kim to share how things were going in their contact center, she said, "It feels like things are hanging on by a thread, and at any moment, it could break."

He asked her to elaborate a little. "Right now, all our contact center metrics are looking good. But it's only because our supervisors are going above and beyond to help out. They have to jump in on almost every call to answer questions, or they need to completely take over the call so it can be resolved. Our supervisors are burned out, and something needs to change. Our approach to training our agents just isn't working."

Buried in a Backlog

In 2022, Dan's department was struggling. His employees couldn't handle the current volume of transactions, and they needed to bring on new employees to try to meet the demand.

But training new employees up to a high level of proficiency usually took months. And until the new hires could perform transactions independently, they were a burden on supervisors and coworkers, slowing things down significantly.

Dan also had to deal with constant change. Procedures got tweaked, information would be updated, and each quarter, Dan's company added new products and locations. It was more than his team could manage, and Dan always felt like he was trying to catch up.

Dan felt like his team was treading water, and he wasn't sure they'd be able to turn things around anytime soon. He needed a solution that could help his team grow and adapt to change.

Crushed by Complexity

Jack's customer service team was responsible for helping patients troubleshoot complex medical devices over the phone. Not an easy task. Fortunately, they had several agents who were very experienced. This allowed them to adequately handle the calls that came in.

When new agents came aboard, these experienced agents would bring the new hires up to speed. That process could take 12–18 months. That was longer than they would like, but they were getting by.

However, in 2020, Jack's customer service team was hit with two major changes that negatively impacted their customer service.

1. Many of their most experienced agents left the team.
2. They had to train agents remotely.

When those experienced agents left, all of the knowledge and experience they had walked right out the door with them.

The company's training program had never been great at preparing agents to work independently. It relied heavily on one-on-one coaching by senior agents. But now, with remote training sessions and fewer agents to provide coaching, it became too much to handle.

There was simply too much information for new agents to absorb. More and more new agents quit before they ever left training. In some cases, agents were so stressed to take their first call that they were in tears.

Jack wasn't sure how they were going to solve this. He needed a solution that could help new employees perform dozens of complex processes without bogging down his more experienced agents.

Everything Feels Broken

Jen's department was in charge of responding to residents in one major U.S. city who had questions about or needed help with their water service. If residents called to ask why their water bill was so high or if new residents called in to have their water turned on, they would have to wait up to two hours for the call to be answered.

When residents did reach a person, it was playing agent roulette. If you got an agent who had been there for several years, they would probably be able to help.

But if you got anyone else with less than 18 months of experience, you were in for an unpleasant ride of incomplete answers and call escalations.

It wasn't the agent's fault. To get the full picture of what could be going on with someone's water bill, you had to navigate multiple screens filled with densely formatted data. It was only after years of experience that an agent could understand which data mattered when researching a customer's question.

Everything felt broken, and the team was demoralized. They weren't even close to offering the level of service they wanted to offer. Her department was like a penitentiary system. People arrived, did their time, and moved on as soon as they could get out.

New hires and complexity don't mix well. It felt like they were trying to build a house of cards on a windy day. Jen needed a way to get a handle on their operating procedures so that employees could do their job.

The Problem: Learning Is Hard When Operations Are Complex

Each of these individuals was faced with the types of challenges that make supervisors, directors, and business owners just want to give up and go home. These aren't the types of problems that are exciting to solve. The constant barrage of questions and problems seems to suck the energy and joy out of everything.

Work becomes miserable when transferring knowledge to your employees is hard, especially when you are trying to transfer operational knowledge.

Operational knowledge is all the knowledge that your employees need to successfully fulfill requests, complete tasks, answer questions, and solve problems. In most organizations, it is the knowledge that can only be acquired by "being" in the business for many months or years.

Every department in your business requires operational knowledge. Customer support, back-office operations, sales, marketing, and finance—all require a mastery of operational knowledge. Operational knowledge can be as simple as "How do I fill out my timecard?" or as complex as "How do I troubleshoot this error code?"

Operational knowledge is black and white—right or wrong. While there can be various opinions about what the right marketing strategy is, the best way to negotiate a deal, or the most effective way to source employees, operational knowledge is clear-cut. The answer an employee gives to a customer is either correct or it isn't. The way an employee processes the returned product is either compliant with your procedures or a total mess. The frontline tech is either applying your policies correctly to a given situation or laying the seeds of confusion and frustration by just winging it.

But there is always someone who knows what the answer is to questions like:

- How do I use the software?
- How do I solve the problem?
- How do I navigate the complexity?

They may be named Lisa, Jose, John, Jake, or Melanie. Or they may even be you. Whatever their name is, they are the person you and everyone else go to when they need guidance on how to handle a particular situation or task.

Learning Takes Too Long

In each of the scenarios I shared at the beginning of this chapter, the problem was that the people who possessed operational knowledge struggled to teach those who didn't. There were employees and supervisors who knew how to handle the complex scenarios and answer the tough questions. But they couldn't effectively teach those skills or that information to new or existing employees in a timely manner.

They tried the typical approaches of classroom lecturing, learning management systems, and shadowing. But those approaches just weren't doing the job, at least, not at a pace that was manageable.

For complex tasks, it would take 12 or more months before employees learned enough to work independently.

Even if the tasks were simple, they would often change and then throw everyone off. Employees would have to unlearn and relearn, and that would often take weeks.

Plus, if you add everything up, the number of steps and decisions, and clicks involved in a business's operations are in the thousands. The sheer volume of information to memorize is enormous.

Why Are Things So Hard? The Convergence of Complexity and Change

Maybe you have felt this way in your business. If you have, it can be hard to put your finger on exactly why things are so hard.

The answer is that you probably have a business that deals with a high degree of complexity and/or change.

Look at the chart below. If your business could be represented by the dot in the lower left corner, low complexity and low change, then put this book down right now. You don't need it.

Defining the Pain

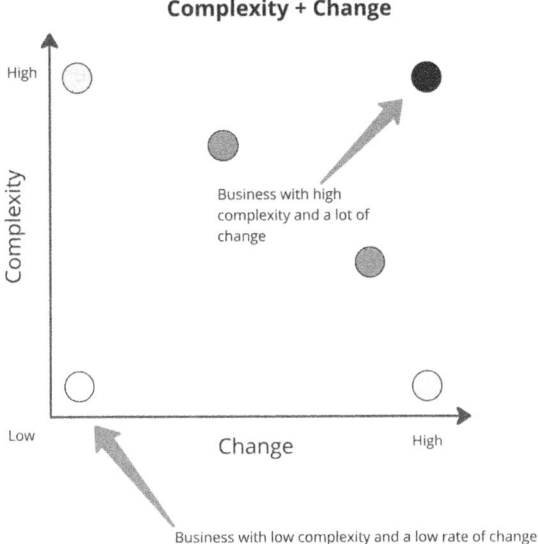

But if you are at the high end of complexity, change, or both, then you know how impossible it feels to help employees be confident, efficient, and independent.

The fact is, you are trying to cram more information into your employees' brains than they were ever designed to hold.

Knowledge Challenges Affect Every Aspect of Your Business

If you look at most customer support issues, the root cause is a lack of knowledge. Low customer satisfaction scores? These are often driven by agents who give wrong or incomplete answers. Long handle times? When agents are unsure what to do, they take longer to resolve calls, resulting in extended hold times for waiting customers. We have seen businesses where their average task time was 70% longer than necessary because of insufficient employee knowledge.

Knowledge challenges affect your training costs. Training can take weeks, months, or even years. These longer training times don't only cost thousands but have also been shown to cause higher rates of new hire attrition.

Lack of knowledge affects compliance. We heard a story about a teller in a regional-sized bank who made a mistake when accepting a deposit. That mistake cost the bank $10,000, and the employee had to be let go. All because of a lack of knowledge.

Knowledge challenges affect your ability to scale your business. They affect your ability to reduce your headcount. It makes outsourcing cumbersome, and it slows down any merger or acquisition.

Knowledge challenges impact your ability to adapt to changes. Small changes, like an extra step in a procedure, or large changes, like a new CRM or ERP system, increase mistakes, cause frustration, and decrease productivity.

Knowledge challenges limit your ability to thrive in a remote or hybrid work environment. Employees who used to be able to turn to their neighbors for assistance are now filling Slack or Teams with endless questions.

Most importantly, a lack of operational knowledge by less-experienced employees puts a huge load on your best and most experienced employees. Instead of spending their time using their experience and knowledge to move the business forward, they fill their days answering questions, fixing mistakes, and putting out fires. Their inability to transfer the knowledge in their heads to less experienced employees ensures both job security and job misery.

Training and Shadowing Don't Work Fast Enough

Companies today each spend thousands of dollars putting on formal training programs to solve these knowledge challenges. These training programs assume that if somebody with knowledge simply explains what to do and shows a PowerPoint slide with bullet points that say the exact same thing, employees will remember what was said and be able to apply it on the job.

Unfortunately, research has shown that most formal training programs don't work.

- Only 25% of respondents to a 2010 McKinsey survey believe that training improved business performance.[1]
- 70% of employees report that they don't have mastery of the skills needed to do their jobs.[2]
- Only 12% of employees apply new skills learned in L&D programs to their jobs.[3]

So businesses mostly rely on shadowing. This is where an employee repeatedly observes another experienced employee performing a job. The assumption is that if an employee watches others long enough, they will eventually know enough to perform the job on their own.

Shadowing is not an effective way to achieve consistency and efficiency.

Then, when employees make mistakes, especially in areas where they have received training, we become frustrated. But these mistakes are not usually born out of a lack of effort. In his book *The Checklist Manifesto*, Atul Gawande describes what it feels like to make a mistake in a complex work environment:

> For those who do the work, however,—the judgment feels like it ignores how extremely difficult the job is. Every day there is more and more to manage and get right and learn. And defeat under conditions of complexity occurs

---

[1] https://www.mckinsey.com/capabilities/people-and-organizational-performance/our-insights/getting-more-from-your-training-programs

[2] https://www.gartner.com/en/human-resources/role/learning-development

[3] https://www.shiftelearning.com/blog/statistics-on-corporate-training-and-what-they-mean-for-your-companys-future

far more often despite great effort rather than from a lack of it.[4]

Employees are trying harder but still failing because expectations are unrealistic. In many situations, employees have received formal training and passed the required assessments, but in the moment they need to apply that knowledge to answer a question, solve a problem, or respond to a request, they fail to do so successfully.

They are being asked to keep too much information in their heads.

Reframing the Problem: Teaching vs. Knowledge Transfer

In his book, *What's Your Problem?*, author and researcher Thomas Wedell-Wedellsborg states:

> *"The way you frame a problem determines which solutions you come up with.*
>
> *"By shifting the way you see the problem— that is, by reframing it—, you can sometimes find radically better solutions."*[5]

Businesses have always framed the problems described so far as "learning problems." And when you have a learning problem, you look for a learning solution.

Learning solutions are focused on cramming information into people's heads and getting people to memorize. But there's a major challenge with this approach when it comes to business

---

[4] Gawande, Atul. *The Checklist Manifesto: How to Get Things Right.* Henry Holt and Co. Kindle Edition, p. 12.

[5] Thomas Wedell-Wedellsborg. *What's Your Problem?: To Solve Your Toughest Problems, Change the Problems You Solve.* Harvard Business Review Press. Kindle Edition, p. 4.

operations. No matter how much information you present to somebody, our brains are like our stomachs—there's only so much we can digest at once. It's what product designers call a gravity problem. Gravity exists, and there's nothing we can do about it. So, any product that is designed must take into account gravity, or else it will flop.

Well, our poor ability to memorize lots of information is a gravity problem. There's nothing we can do about it. So, if you need employees to learn … er … memorize thousands of clicks and steps and complex processes (and then unlearn and relearn them when operations change), it's going to be a long and messy process.

But what if we reframe the learning problem? What if instead of viewing the problem as "employees need to memorize a bunch of complex tasks and information that will change on a quarterly basis," we framed the problem as "employees need to *do* a bunch of complex tasks that may be changed on a quarterly basis"?

What if we weren't so hung up on cramming more information into employees' heads? What if, instead, we were focused on transferring knowledge to the employee in the moment they needed it—right when they performed a task, answered a question, or responded to a request?

What if we didn't actually need employees to memorize any of the operational details in order to be proficient at performing the operational tasks?

When we reframe the problem from a *learning* problem to a *knowledge transfer* problem, we open up a whole new world of possible solutions. When we remove the constraints of memorization, we open up performance improvements that would be otherwise impossible.

What Happens When We Reframe the Problem

Kim, Dan, Jack, and Jen all reframed the problem. They stopped trying to teach employees more information and instead focused on solving the knowledge transfer problem.

What were the results?

Kim's supervisors are no longer burned out. Agents are up and running and independent in less than one month.

Dan's new hires are hitting their performance targets and are no longer a drain on their more experienced counterparts. Their time to proficiency went from five months down to 30 days. Employee productivity has more than doubled—including the productivity of new hires.

Jack removed all the tears from training. His team standardized and optimized the troubleshooting process and saved their business $2.3 million in one year.

Jen reduced time to proficiency from 12 months to less than 30 days, and call wait times have been reduced by more than 90 minutes. Her gloomy work environment became a place where people actually smile. Instead of trying to find a way out, people now want to be part of her organization. She said, "This is the greatest human experiment I have ever been a part of."

That is the purpose of this book—to help you solve the knowledge transfer problem and transform your work environment just like Kim, Dan, Jack, and Jen.

To accomplish that, we are going to present you with a new framework for transferring knowledge.

That framework is called Find & Follow.

Summary

- Learning operational knowledge is hard, especially in environments that deal with a lot of complexity and/or change.
- Training and shadowing don't help employees work independently and efficiently.
- By reframing the "learning" problem as a "knowledge transfer" problem and focusing on a knowledge transfer solution, we can make dramatic improvements to performance.

In the next chapter, we are going to help you see how familiar you already are with the principles behind Find & Follow. You just never experience them at work.

Chapter 2:

You Have Already Experienced Find & Follow

In this chapter, you will:

- Learn the basic premise of the Find & Follow Framework
- See examples of how you have already experienced it in real life
- See how Find & Follow can be applied to the work environment

The premise behind Find & Follow is simple. Instead of learning mountains of Operational Knowledge, employees will find digital guides that they will follow to respond to requests, perform tasks, answer questions, and solve problems. In Find & Follow, the knowledge is transferred to the employee right in the moment they need it.

We do this by:

- Separating foundational knowledge and actionable knowledge
- Teaching foundational knowledge
- Providing recipes for actionable knowledge that are findable, followable, and scannable

We will explain each of these aspects in greater detail in later chapters. At this point, I just want you to realize that you have already experienced this method of learning. Let me share a few examples.

Using Find & Follow to Cook a Turkey

Friends invite my family and me over to a dinner party and ask us to bring a cooked turkey. I've never done that before, so what do I do? A week before the party, I go to YouTube, and I find a 10-minute video of Gordon Ramsay showing the process of cooking a turkey. I also find a printed version of the recipe.

I watch the 10-minute video and feel comfortable with what the process will look like.

On the day of the party, I pull up the recipe and follow it.

The turkey turns out great, and I'm a hero for that evening.

Notice that I didn't have to attend culinary school to make a delicious turkey. I'm not a culinary expert. All I needed to do was find a resource that gave me a foundational understanding of the context and the process (the video) and a resource that gave me step-by-step instructions (the recipe). The results? A delicious meal.

That's Find & Follow. Gordon Ramsay was able to efficiently transfer his knowledge to me in a way that was easy to find (YouTube and a Google Search) and Follow (printed recipe), allowing me to create a delicious meal.

I don't have to memorize the recipe. Any time I want to cook a turkey, I can find it and follow it.

Find & Follow and Trampolines

The weather is warming up, and my kids and my wife are asking to get a trampoline. Their cousins have one, and we all think it will be a great way to get the kids outside to burn off some energy.

I purchase a trampoline from Dick's Sporting Goods and bring it home. Since I already know what a trampoline is and what the end product will look like, I have a good foundational understanding. I don't need to pull up a video or get any kind of explanation. I can go right to the instructions.

I pull out the pieces of the trampoline and open the instruction pamphlet. Within 2.5 hours, I've got a trampoline set up. (Admittedly, your trampoline assembly experience may have been more painful than mine, as not all manuals are created equally. More on this later in the book.)

That's Find & Follow. The trampoline manufacturers were able to efficiently transfer their actionable knowledge to me in a way that I could easily find it and follow it. I'm not a trampoline expert, but that day I acted like one.

And now I know a lot more about putting a trampoline together because I did it.

Find & Follow in the Workplace

How can we apply those same principles of knowledge transfer in the workplace? Let's look at some examples.

A new employee was hired at the local credit union. They will be a teller.

The new employee will have to answer questions like, "How do I set up direct deposit?"

The new employee has never done that before and isn't familiar with what direct deposit is.

So, the employee watches 10 minutes of videos that explain some foundational concepts: what direct deposit is, who uses it, when they might ask this question, and what the direct deposit process looks like from a high level.

The employee also is shown a digital guide that provides very clear instructions for how to set up direct deposit.

When a customer walks into the credit union and asks how to set up direct deposit, the employee searches their internal knowledge base like they would if they were using Google, pulls up the digital guide, and follows it to respond to the customer.

The exchange is handled perfectly, and both the employee and the customer are thrilled by how easy it was.

That is Find & Follow. The subject matter experts were able to efficiently transfer their foundational knowledge so the teller understood the context. They were then able to transfer their actionable knowledge to the teller in a way that was easy to find (searchable knowledge base) and follow (a digital guide that had very clear instructions).

In the future, the teller will be able to handle all questions in the same way. They will not have to memorize all the details because they can find the digital guide and follow it each and every time.

How about a more experienced employee who has worked at the credit union for two years? They are asked how to deposit a check on the credit union's mobile app.

The employee has never done this before; however, they are familiar with the concept of depositing checks, and they are familiar with the mobile app. Since they already have foundational knowledge, they don't need to watch any videos or read up on any background information.

The employee can search the credit union's knowledge base, just like they would in Google, and pull up a digital guide that walks through the steps of depositing a check on the mobile app.

You Have Already Experienced Find & Follow

That is Find & Follow.

Even though the employee had never done the task before, the subject matter experts were able to efficiently transfer their knowledge using a digital guide.

There's no need for the employee to memorize all the steps. In the future, when a customer asks the same question, the employee can find the digital guide and follow the steps.

Scan the QR code below to see a video example of what it looks like to find and follow digital guides.

www.screensteps.com/find-follow-book/resources/find-and-follow-example

Summary

- Find & Follow is a framework that helps you transfer knowledge more quickly.
- The framework first helps you separate foundational knowledge from actionable knowledge.
- It then guides you in how to teach foundational knowledge quickly and deliver effective digital guides to transfer actionable knowledge.
- We already experience the principles of Find & Follow in our personal lives when we follow a recipe or assemble a product.
- Find & Follow helps us bring those same knowledge transfer experiences into our workplaces.
- Find & Follow was developed by working very closely in real-world situations and assembling best practices into a comprehensive and repeatable framework.

We will soon dive into the details of the Find & Follow Framework, but first, we need to help you assess how efficiently your business is currently transferring knowledge. To do that, we are going introduce a concept called Knowledge Operations.

Part II:

Knowledge Operations

"Efficiency is intelligent laziness."
– Anonymous

Chapter 3:

Measuring Where You Are At—The Knowledge Ops Maturity Model

In this chapter, you will learn:

- What the Knowledge Ops Maturity Model is
- The 5 stages of the model
- How to determine which stage your organization is operating in

How Efficiently Do You Transfer Knowledge?

Have you ever stopped to ask yourself how your business uses the knowledge that you have? Most haven't. They may start a documentation initiative, or they may commit to providing better training. But they don't look at how employees actually use knowledge to do their jobs.

Capturing and teaching knowledge doesn't drive value. Using knowledge does.

By assessing how efficiently your business transfers knowledge, you can get a clearer picture of why knowledge transfer feels difficult in your business and what steps you can take to make the transfer of knowledge more efficient.

The Knowledge Ops Maturity Model

The Knowledge Ops Maturity Model is a tool for helping you assess how effectively your organization transfers and uses knowledge. Your knowledge ops (or knowledge operations) consist of the technologies and behaviors that your team uses to transfer knowledge.

The Knowledge Ops Maturity Model helps you identify how mature your organization is at transferring knowledge from those who have operational knowledge to those who don't. It can help you diagnose why achieving a high level of effectiveness can feel so difficult in your business and communicate to your whole team what improvements you would like to make.

Measuring Where You Are At—The Knowledge Ops Maturity Model

Knowledge Ops Maturity Model

Employee Independence ↑

1. Tribal
All training happens through shadowing and asking a supervisor/co-worker for help.

No documentation exists.

2. Document
Some documentation exists but it isn't regularly used or is not used effectively.

Documentation is not designed with the end-user's needs in mind.

3. Guide
Digital guides are designed to guide employees when completing tasks, solving problems, and making decisions.

Employees use the digital guides each time they perform a task.

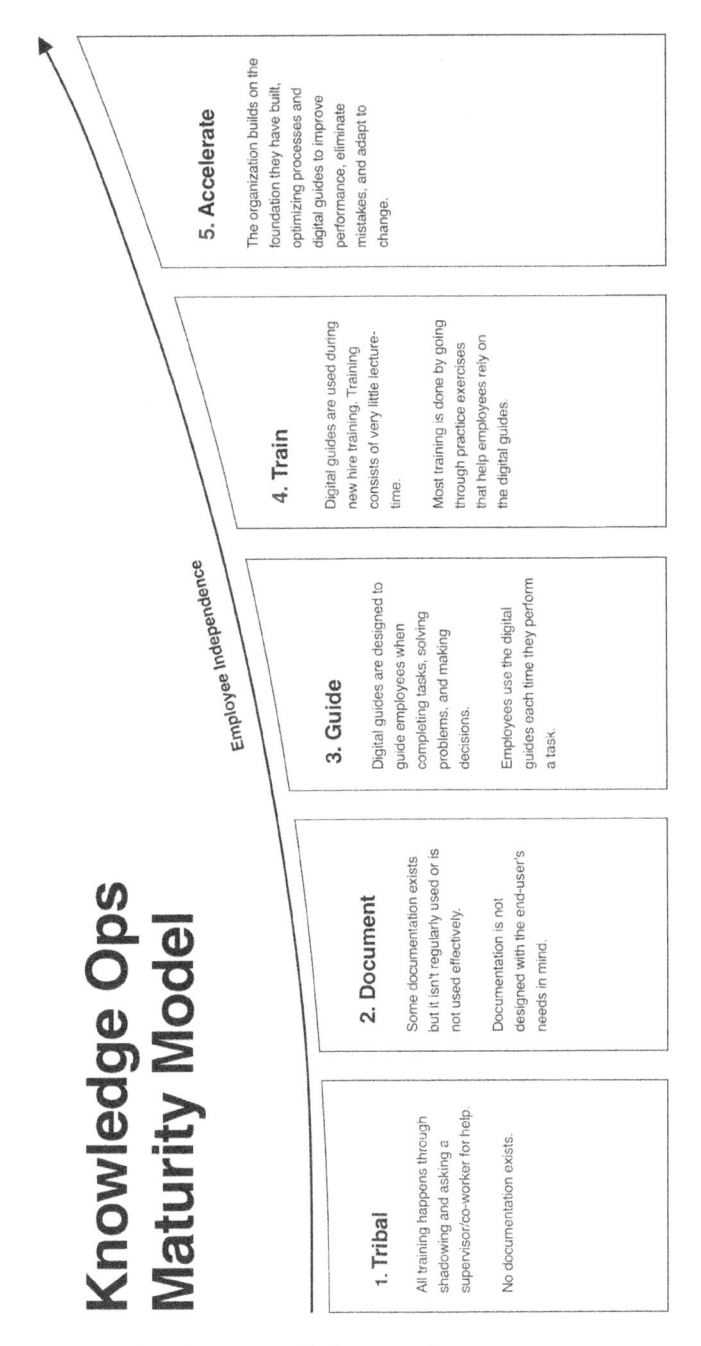

4. Train
Digital guides are used during new hire training. Training consists of very little lecture-time.

Most training is done by going through practice exercises that help employees rely on the digital guides.

5. Accelerate
The organization builds on the foundation they have built, optimizing processes and digital guides to improve performance, eliminate mistakes, and adapt to change.

You can download a PDF of this graphic at www.screensteps.com/find-follow-book/resources

A Few Definitions

Before we explain the model, it will help if we define a few terms that you'll see in this book.

Tribal Knowledge: Any knowledge that resides only in employees' heads, their email archives, or Slack/Team messages. Tribal knowledge requires employees to work from memory or by asking a co-worker/supervisor.

Documented Knowledge: Any knowledge that is written down somewhere (besides emails and chat messages). Just because it is documented doesn't mean that it is usable or that it gets used. If documented knowledge doesn't get used, then employees still have to rely on their memories in their daily work.

Actionable Knowledge: Knowledge or information that is required to perform a task, answer a question, make a decision, or solve a problem.

Foundational Knowledge: Background or contextual knowledge that must be understood in order to successfully apply actionable knowledge. This is also called domain knowledge.

Documentation: This is anything that is written down in a formal article or document. Documentation is typically found in Word, PDF documents, PowerPoint decks, flowcharts, knowledge bases, or wikis.

Knowledge Base Articles: These are articles that are in an online knowledge base. They are NOT Word, PDF, or PowerPoint files. They are created in an online article editor and may contain images or videos. Users typically find these articles via an online knowledge base or wiki.

Digital Guides: These are like knowledge base articles but have more interactive elements like decision trees, checklists, expandable sections, pop-up links, and "click to continue" buttons. These elements allow information to be communicated gradually and more clearly. The main difference between a knowledge base article and a digital guide is that a digital guide will guide an employee through a process or procedure by just presenting the level of detail they need in that moment.

The 5 Stages of the Knowledge Ops Maturity Model

Alright, now let's jump back into the five stages of the Knowledge Ops Maturity Model. The purpose of these stages is to help you identify where you currently are and where you want to be.

Remember, this isn't just about what technology you have. It is about how people behave in your business as they try to transfer knowledge.

The 5 stages are:

1. Tribal
2. Document
3. Guide
4. Train
5. Accelerate

In the lower stages (1-2), organizations rely on tribal knowledge to perform their work.

Find & Follow

The Knowledge Ops Maturity Model

Stage 5: Accelerate	The organization builds on the foundation they have built, optimizing processes and digital guides to improve performance, eliminate mistakes, and adapt to change.
Stage 4: Train	Digital guides are used during new hire training. Training consists of very little lecture-time. Most training is done through practice activities that help employees rely on the digital guides.
Stage 3: Guide	Digital guides are designed to guide employees when completing tasks, solving problems, and making decisions. Employee use the digital guides each time they perform a task.
Stage 2: Document	Some documentation exists, but it isn't regularly used or is not used effectively. Documentation is not designed with the end-user's needs in mind.
Stage 1: Tribal	All training happens through shadowing or asking a supervisor/co-worker for help. No documentation exists.

As you move up the stages (3-5), you begin to rely less on tribal knowledge and more on digital guides that transfer actionable knowledge instantly.

The Knowledge Ops Maturity Model

Stage 5: Accelerate	The organization builds on the foundation they have built, optimizing processes and digital guides to improve performance, eliminate mistakes, and adapt to change.
Stage 4: Train	Digital guides are used during new hire training. Training consists of very little lecture-time. Most training is done through practice activities that help employees rely on the digital guides.
Stage 3: Guide	Digital guides are designed to guide employees when completing tasks, solving problems, and making decisions. Employee use the digital guides each time they perform a task.
Stage 2: Document	Some documentation exists, but it isn't regularly used or is not used effectively. Documentation is not designed with the end-user's needs in mind.
Stage 1: Tribal	All training happens through shadowing or asking a supervisor/co-worker for help. No documentation exists.

Tribal Stage companies rely almost completely on word-of-mouth, shadowing, and digging through old emails or chat conversations. Nothing is formally documented or organized, and very little is consistent.

Companies at the **Document Stage** have some documentation, but it doesn't drive the results they need. Either employees don't use the documentation at all, or they aren't able to use it successfully. The documentation can't "stand-alone," so the employee has to turn to co-workers or supervisors for help.

Because employees can't or won't use the documentation, they resort to relying on their memories or tribal knowledge.

At the **Guide Stage**, employees don't work from memory, and they don't rely on tribal knowledge. The organization has developed a culture where everyone uses digital guides to assist them. Every time they perform a task or troubleshoot a problem of any complexity, employees pull up digital guides filled with actionable knowledge so they can work independently, efficiently, and without mistakes.

At the **Train Stage**, companies have separated out foundational knowledge and actionable knowledge, and they have built training systems that effectively transfer each type of knowledge. For example, employees may take a course to learn the what, why, and when behind a particular set of processes. Then, employees learn how to use the digital guides for performing those processes in their day-to-day work.

New hires are onboarded quickly and efficiently, and cross-training can happen in hours instead of weeks. Training time not only decreases, but employees leave training with the power to immediately perform their job independently and efficiently. Shadowing is no longer needed.

Finally, at the **Accelerate Stage**, businesses have the foundation in place to optimize and adapt to change.

Improvements can be rolled out in minutes instead of weeks. New systems and processes can be adopted without any negative impact on productivity. Supervisors and employees can work together to optimize processes and improve the business.

Identifying Where You Are at on the Model

Let's look at each stage in detail. As we explain each stage, try to honestly assess where your team is at.

Stage 1: Tribal

At the Tribal Stage, organizations rely completely on tribal knowledge. Tribal knowledge is where information is passed by word of mouth (either verbally or through chat and email). For example, co-workers ask each other how to answer a question, complete a task, or solve a problem.

New employees are trained by listening to lectures, shadowing other employees, asking questions, and making a lot of mistakes. Supervisors spend most of their time answering those questions and fixing those mistakes. Employees do not feel confident working on their own.

At this stage, it takes employees between 3–18 months (if they last that long) to feel comfortable performing operational tasks independently.

Key Indicators Your Organization Is at Stage 1

How do you know if your organization is at the Tribal Stage?

You have no documentation. When your employees have questions, they have to ask their supervisors or co-workers for answers. There are no guides they can reference for help.

Your company has no centralized location for information. Typically, this means your employees need to search a variety of different applications to find resources. They might find an answer in chat messages, emails, shared folders, etc.

Key employees have to work overtime and are never able to take a true vacation.

Everything feels chaotic, and employees feel stressed. Some organizations have told us that they feel like operations are hanging by a thread or that they're constantly bailing water out of the boat just to stay afloat. It feels like any new challenge or change could sink the ship.

Stage 2: Document

At the Document Stage, organizations start to document their systems, policies, and procedures. But the documentation that is created is focused on capturing information or answering basic questions instead of enabling performance. The documentation is either too long, too incomplete, too complicated to understand, or too impossible to find when employees actually need it.

Because the documentation can't stand on its own, nobody uses it on a regular basis because, in the end, they still need the assistance of supervisors or subject matter experts to help them complete a task or solve a problem.

Documentation in this stage may reside in Word, PDF, PowerPoint, Visio, or Excel files that are hard to search and even more difficult to read.

Or maybe the organization has an online knowledge base, but even if employees find the right article, they encounter massive walls of text that are difficult to understand and apply.

> Scan the QR code below to see examples of what documentation typically looks like in the Document Stage.
>
> www.screensteps.com/find-follow-book/resources/document-stage-examples

We also find that in this stage, documentation isn't designed to deal with all of the complexity or variables that are part of the organization's procedures, nor is it designed to be used by employees with different experience levels. The documentation either has too much detail for an experienced user or too little detail for a new employee.

In this stage, a lot of knowledge has been captured, but it hasn't been designed or operationalized. It is like having flour, eggs, and milk, convincing yourself that having those ingredients is the same as having a cake, and then wondering why no one will eat it.

Key Indicators Your Organization Is at Stage 2

If you are in the Document Stage, you most likely have a lot of documentation, but it is rarely used. The documentation consists of massive amounts of text, hour-long recorded webinars, and large PowerPoint files.

It's difficult to know how or even if your employees are using your guides. You either don't have access to usage analytics, or you don't use analytics to inform your decisions.

Or maybe employees are trying to use your documentation, but they aren't doing so successfully. They read documentation and either still make mistakes or have to reach out to someone else for assistance.

Another sign you are at the Document Stage is that your documentation is outdated or has broken links, but nobody notices. Employees don't recognize that your documentation is outdated and inaccurate because they never use it.

If employees read your documentation and say, "My head hurts," then you are at the Document Stage.

Stage 3: Guide

The Guide Stage documents the actionable knowledge (i.e., how things are done) in your operations. But instead of just dumping information into a document, organizations operating at the Guide Stage design digital guides that guide employees through every task and interaction.

Also, there is a change in how resources are used. Employees don't just pull up documentation when they get stuck. The organization has a culture where everyone follows digital guides to help them:

- Complete tasks, answer questions, and solve problems independently.
- Work confidently.
- Achieve proficiency quickly.
- Adapt to changes immediately.

The digital guides are designed to effectively transfer knowledge, no matter how basic or complex that knowledge is. These digital guides can take the form of articles, interactive checklists, or decision trees. We will explain these types of guides in detail later on in the book.

Because they are no longer relying on the limited and imperfect memories of their employees, organizations operating at the Guide Stage are more agile, consistent, and efficient.

Scan the QR code below to see an example of what digital guides in the Guide Stage can look like.

[QR code]

www.screensteps.com/find-follow-book/resources/guide-stage-examples

---

In some departments, the Guide Stage may sound like it's excessive. And if employees are only doing a handful of simple transactions over and over again, it might be. But if you are working in an organization where there is high change, high complexity, or both, then the Guide Stage will transform your culture and your metrics.

Key Indicators Your Organization Is at Stage 3

At the Guide Stage, your employees are able to handle simple or complex tasks without supervisor assistance. Employees perform tasks efficiently and confidently. They make little to no mistakes.

However, in this stage, training is still taking a long time (more than a month). There is still a lot of shadowing and nesting that goes on for new hires.

Stage 4: Train

The Train Stage goes beyond just creating resources for transferring actionable knowledge by also creating resources for transferring foundational knowledge. Organizations leverage both types of resources when doing new hire training and cross-training.

This results in employees achieving proficiency quickly and confidently when learning how to do something new.

Imagine you are training new cooks at a restaurant that has no recipes. They would have to memorize the ingredients and nuances of each dish. That would be a hard restaurant to work in!

At the Train Stage, we make sure all our "chefs":

1. Have the necessary foundational knowledge for the jobs they'll be doing (e.g., the "what"), and
2. Know how to use the recipes to do their jobs.

Once you've reached the Train Stage, you use a repeatable training program to teach employees the foundational knowledge they need to do their jobs and then teach employees how to use your digital guides to actually perform those jobs. We call this creating a Training Factory.

Instead of sitting through hours, days, and weeks of lectures and PowerPoints, new hires spend a little time learning some foundational principles and then spend the bulk of training time practicing how to use the company's digital guides to handle realistic scenarios.

Key Indicators Your Organization Is at Stage 4

At the Train Stage, businesses have built a repeatable training system that can produce consistent results. The confidence in new hires soars while their time to proficiency plummets. New hires become knowledgeable, consistent, independent, and efficient in less than 30 days from their start date.

Employees that are changing roles can become proficient even faster since they usually already have the requisite foundational knowledge and can jump straight to learning how to use the digital guides for their new job function.

Stage 5: Accelerate

Once organizations reach the Train Stage, they are already working extremely efficiently.

The last step is to advance to the Accelerate Stage, where performance continues to accelerate as existing processes and guides are optimized and improved. Because employees rely on the digital guides, they instantly adapt to new best practices or improved procedures.

Key Indicators Your Organization Is at Stage 5

At this stage, your company doesn't just have effective guides and use them. Your team is analyzing and optimizing your processes. You reduce task times, remove bottlenecks, and achieve major cost savings.

Your team no longer fears change. It embraces it, constantly evolving to improve the business.

Overestimating How Well You Are Doing

We find that most organizations overestimate where they are sitting on the model. They make the mistake of measuring what knowledge resources they think they have and not assessing how employees are using them.

Here are a few questions to ask yourself to assess where you are at on the model:

- What happens when an employee has questions? What do they do?
    - Do they ask their co-worker or supervisor for assistance? If so, you are at the Tribal Stage.

- Do they look for information in your knowledge base but are unable to find what they need or use the knowledge base to do the job independently? Then you are at the Document Stage.
  - Are they able to find a digital guide and use it without any assistance to answer their question or solve their problem? Then you are at the Guide Stage or higher.
- When an employee performs a task that has some level of complexity, what do they do?
  - If they work from memory or ask for assistance, you are at the Tribal or Document Stage.
  - If they follow a digital guide, then you are at the Guide Stage or higher.

The Knowledge Ops Maturity Model

Stage	Employee Behavior
Stage 5: Accelerate	Using digital guides
Stage 4: Train	
Stage 3: Guide	
Stage 2: Document	Working from memory
Stage 1: Tribal	

- When an employee is being trained, are they taught to use the digital guides, and do they practice using those digital guides?
  - If yes, then you are at the Train or Accelerate Stage.
  - If no, then you are in the Guide Stage or lower.

The Knowledge Ops Maturity Model

Stage	Employee Behavior
Stage 5: Accelerate	
Stage 4: Train	Learn to use guides during training
Stage 3: Guide	Only use guides while working
Stage 2: Document	
Stage 1: Tribal	

- Are supervisors or trainers targeting specific procedures and optimizing the guides until they decrease task times or error rates *without* requiring additional employee training?
    - If yes, then you are working at the Accelerate Stage.
    - If no, then you are at the Train Stage or lower.

The Knowledge Ops Maturity Model

Stage	Employee Behavior
Stage 5: Accelerate	
Stage 4: Train	Learn to use guides during training
Stage 3: Guide	Only use guides while working
Stage 2: Document	
Stage 1: Tribal	

Measuring Where You Are At—The Knowledge Ops Maturity Model

- Do supervisors and employees have the bandwidth to recognize opportunities to improve business operations and implement those changes?
    - If yes, then you are at the Accelerate Stage.
    - If no, then you are at one of the other stages.

Scan this QR code to take a free assessment and measure where your team is at on the Knowledge Ops Maturity Model.

www.screensteps.com/find-follow-book/resources/maturity-grader

> **Summary**
> - The Knowledge Ops Maturity Model can help organizations understand how effectively they transfer operational knowledge to their employees.
> - Most organizations overestimate which stage they are at in the model.
> - You need to look at what your employees actually do when they are working to accurately determine which stage you are operating at.

Now that you can successfully identify which stage you are operating at let's look at the benefits of moving up to the higher stages of the model.

Chapter 4:

The Benefits of Moving Up the Knowledge Ops Maturity Model

In this chapter, you will learn:

- How operating at stages 3, 4, and 5 of the Knowledge Ops Maturity Model will impact your costs, operations, and culture
- How operating at these higher stages prepares your team to react to change

When you stop relying on tribal knowledge and start operating at the higher levels of the Knowledge Ops Maturity Model, everything about your business changes. In this chapter, we are going to highlight how these changes will impact your costs, operations, and culture.

We will break this down into three areas:

- Cost and operations
- Culture
- Change readiness

The Impact on Cost and Operations

The speed at which you transfer knowledge in your organization has a major economic impact. Inefficient or ineffective knowledge transfer, at the very least, makes everything take longer, driving up costs significantly. At its worst, poor knowledge transfer causes mistakes and non-compliance, leading to unhappy clients or regulatory problems.

When you operate at the Guide, Train, and Accelerate stages, you reduce training and performance costs and lower the risk of non-compliance.

Let's look at several areas where costs and risk are impacted:

- New employee onboarding
- Customer service
- Compliance
- Average task time

TESTING KNOWLEDGE TRANSFER ON THE FRONT LINES—THE CONTACT CENTER

While the benefits of faster knowledge transfer can apply across all areas of your organization, you will see that many of the stories and statistics I present will be from contact centers we have worked with.

Why?

The contact center is the frontline of knowledge management and performance.

Many contact centers measure key metrics such as training time, time to proficiency, average handle time, quality scores, customer satisfaction, and many others. This wealth of data allows us to more accurately measure the impact of knowledge transfer on a business.

- Contact centers often have to engage in the same types of back-office work as other areas in your organization. If we can enable a contact center agent to use your billing system, then we can also empower your accounting team to work independently.
- Contact center agents *have* to use knowledge to do their jobs. They answer questions, respond to requests, and have to troubleshoot problems. A busy contact center will have more opportunities to use knowledge throughout the day than anywhere else in the organization.
- Contact center agents have to use knowledge in high-pressure situations. When you are talking to someone on the other side of the phone, you need to find answers as quickly as possible. Unlike a back-office worker, a contact center agent cannot stop in the middle of a call to watch a video or read a 40-page manual.

The contact center is like the New York City of knowledge transfer. If you can make it there, you can make it anywhere.

So, while many of the examples I will show in this book come from contact centers, please realize that you can see these same improvements across other roles in your organization. Other employees have to answer questions, complete tasks, and solve problems, but their productivity isn't measured as carefully as it is in the contact center.

New Employee Onboarding

Being onboarded into an organization that relies on tribal knowledge is painful for everyone involved. New hires feel lost and confused. Mentors waste time explaining and re-explaining the same things over and over again. And supervisors aren't sure what to do with this person who is incapable of working on their own.

But when a new employee can rely on actionable knowledge, they onboard more quickly, feel more confident, and add value to the organization almost immediately.

We have worked with clients where it would take 12–18 months for new employees to reach a state where they could work independently. Once they stopped relying on tribal knowledge, those times dropped to less than three months. These transformational success stories took place in businesses that had highly complex contact centers.

Here are some numbers from clients who worked in less complicated contact centers:

- Dropped onboarding time from 60 days to less than 7
- Dropped onboarding time from 5 weeks to 3 days

Those numbers sound astonishing, and they are. Many people think that I have misspoken when I share them, but I promise you, that is not a typo. The only thing that changed was where they were on the Knowledge Ops Maturity Model. They moved from the Documentation Stage to the Train Stage.

To quantify that a bit, the table below shows a rough estimate of cost savings in relation to reduced training times. The calculations are based on an hourly cost of $20/hour.

Reduction in onboarding days	Savings per employee onboarded	Savings when onboarding 10 employees	Savings when onboarding 50 employees
53	$8,480	$84,800	$424,000
22	$3,520	$35,200	$176,000
230	$36,800	$368,000	$1,840,000

Customer Service

Customer Service organizations that move up the Knowledge Operations Maturity Model see dramatic improvements:

- Customers get consistent answers.
- Quality scores go up.
- Handle times decrease.
- Escalations decrease.
- NPS and CSAT increase.
- New hire attrition rates drop.

We worked with one group that had to launch a brand-new contact center with agents and supervisors who had no prior product or domain knowledge.

Thirty days after they launched, they were hitting 90% service levels and had quality scores of 98%. They were operating at the Train Stage.

Here are some other results we have seen:

- NPS (Net Promoter Score) boosted by 15 points after they moved to the Guide Stage
- SLA improved by 40% after moving to the Train Stage
- Dramatic reduction in customer complaints after they moved to the Train Stage

Compliance

Being compliant in a tribal knowledge organization is almost impossible. How can you perform to a standard when that standard is stuck in someone's head?

Compliance is crucial in healthcare, finance, and other highly regulated industries, but still, many of these organizations primarily rely on tribal knowledge to perform their jobs.

This results in everyone doing the same thing in different ways, creating a compliance nightmare.

We worked with a contact center that had to troubleshoot medical devices over the phone. While they had documented protocols for troubleshooting the devices, they discovered that none of their agents were following the protocols. Each agent had their own system for troubleshooting the devices, and none of them were compliant with the official procedure.

After they moved to the Guide Stage, everyone started following the same process. They were able to achieve perfect compliance with their procedures.

This increase in compliance reduced unnecessary product returns, contributing to $2.3 million of savings in one year.

Our clients have used the Find & Follow Framework to improve compliance in healthcare and financial organizations as well.

Average Task Time

When we tell people that they should have employees follow digital guides *every* time they take a call or perform a procedure, they almost always think that it will slow down their more experienced employees.

The data shows the opposite.

There is a saying that originates from the Navy SEALs that goes, "Slow is smooth, and smooth is fast."

While we aren't talking about special ops teams, the same principle applies.

In almost every contact center we have worked with, experienced agents resist moving up the maturity model to the Guide Stage. They say it will just slow them down. They can work more quickly from their memories.

And then new hires start outperforming them—by a lot.

In one contact center, tenured agents typically handled about 30 calls per shift. These tenured agents were operating at the Documentation Stage. New hires began operating at the Guide Stage and were able to handle 70–80 calls per shift. Their productivity was more than twice that of the tenured agents.

This same pattern has played out at other contact centers, with new hires handling 2-3 times as many calls as tenured agents.

Employees who follow digital guides every time complete tasks and solve problems in less time.

Impacted Metrics

I have mentioned some of these metrics above, but I will restate them here. These metrics show the breadth of the impact that efficient knowledge transfer can have on your business. With efficient knowledge transfer, you can:

- Decrease average task time
- Reduce the number of escalations
- Cut troubleshooting time by 50% or more
- Cut new hire training time by more than half
- Reduce time to proficiency (the time from when an employee leaves training to when they can work independently) by as much as 90%
- Almost completely eliminate shadowing time (the time employees spend observing other, more experienced employees)
- Boost NPS and CSAT scores
- Improve Quality scores
- Lower new hire attrition rates
- Decrease unnecessary product returns or field service visits caused by inaccurate troubleshooting

The most important cost savings metric to note is that a business will be able to get more done with fewer employees, resulting in significant payroll savings.

The Impact on Culture

Beyond the metrics, there is a significant impact on culture. Here is how several clients have described the change from working at the Tribal Stage to the Train Stage.

> "This has changed everything about how we work. It has been transformative."

> "We took a contact center where everything felt really, really hard, and now it is an easy place to work."

> "Our reps are more confident handling calls on their own. They feel empowered to provide answers without needing to always check with supervisors."

> "Everything is very transparent, and it's very easy to understand what other departments do."

> "Before, reps hated working these calls because everything was just so complicated. Now, everything feels so much easier."

You will see the following changes in your company culture as you adopt Find & Follow:

- Less stress
- Increased confidence
- Increased transparency
- Increased accountability

Less Stress

The decrease in stress is dramatic for organizations operating at the Guide Stage or higher.

Employees experience less stress as they are able to work independently and confidently.

Supervisors experience less stress as they no longer need to constantly answer questions and fix mistakes.

Trainers experience less stress as they shift from lecturing and cramming to facilitating and enabling.

Less stress leads to greater productivity and increased employee retention.

We had one client who provided outsourced services to multiple businesses. They took a client program where everyone was quitting and turned it into the most popular program among their team by moving from the Documentation Stage to the Train Stage.

Increased Confidence

When employees are unsure of what to do, it kills their confidence. The story below shows the impact the higher stages of the Knowledge Ops Maturity Model can have on employee confidence.

We had a client that for years had operated at the Tribal Stage. It would take up to a year for a new employee to be confident enough to analyze the data necessary to answer common customer questions.

But all of that changed in late 2022. Instead of teaching agents to memorize mountains of information, the contact center leaders designed digital guides that agents could find and follow to handle even the most complex situations.

And that is what Mary was using when she took her first call of the morning.

She had dealt with these calls before, and she dreaded them. She never could answer all the customer questions, and she always had to escalate the call to a senior agent. This made her feel inadequate, and she knew that it frustrated the customer on the other end of the phone.

She was just about to escalate the call when her supervisor encouraged her to use the digital guide.

The call was just as complex as it had been before, but the digital guide showed her exactly which questions to ask and which information screens to analyze. The guide was like a coach helping her navigate each stage of the call. Slowly and steadily, she answered every question and navigated every change.

At the end of the call, she stood up, twirled around, put her hand in the air, and cried, "I did it on my own!"

Her confidence was through the roof.

Other clients who are operating at the Train Stage have told us that after just a few days of training, their employees are eager to start taking calls or performing tasks.

This is because clarity creates confidence. Moving up the Knowledge Ops Maturity Model will increase the confidence of everyone on your team.

Increased Accountability

In a tribal knowledge organization, it is impossible to hold anyone accountable. There is just too much ambiguity about how things should be done.

In contrast, at the Guide Stage, employees are accountable for following the digital guides every time, and the knowledge operations team is accountable for ensuring the guides are findable, followable, and correct.

We had one client who was training a group of new hires in their contact center. One new hire was performing way above expectations, while the other was floundering. Both said that they were following the digital guides. But when their supervisor looked at the analytics in the knowledge base software, they found that the star employee had viewed hundreds of digital guides over the last few weeks while the underperforming employee had only looked at three.

Guide Stage organizations can hold their employees accountable for using knowledge correctly.

The Impact on Change Readiness

Some changes are big. Some are small. But all cause disruption and, at least temporarily, negatively impact performance.

There are two primary types of change:

- Adaptive
- Transformational

Adaptive changes are small, incremental changes the organization needs to make to respond to challenges that come up on a daily, weekly, or monthly basis. It is like a cyclist with a pre-determined destination that has to steer around an object in the road, take a detour, or stop and repair a flat tire. The goal of adaptive change is to get back on the road to your destination as quickly as possible.

Examples of adaptive change might be a small software update, a temporary office closing at a medical practice, regulation changes that affect an existing loan processing procedure, or a minor software update. These changes can be temporary, or they may be permanent, but they can cause a lot of confusion and mistakes when not handled correctly.

Transformational change, on the other hand, is a major change. It is like a cyclist who plots out a brand-new destination or decides to trade their bike for a motorcycle. The goal is either to arrive at a better destination or to find a way to get to the same destination faster.

Examples of transformational change could be a new CRM or ERP system, bringing on an outsourcing partner, opening a new location, acquiring a new business, or adopting a remote/hybrid work environment.

Transformational change is hard, and getting it wrong can become very expensive very quickly.

Knowledge Operations and Change Readiness

Change Readiness is a measure of how prepared your organization is to adapt to any given change, whether it be adaptive or transformational.

The faster you can transfer knowledge, the higher your Change Readiness score will be.

Imagine that all the traffic patterns in your city are going to change. If you already have a GPS, then you will be able to adapt very quickly. But if you are just working from a paper map, you will struggle to adapt to the new routes.

Let's look at how Guide, Train, and Accelerate organizations deal with both adaptive and transformational change.

Adaptive Change

We once worked with a customer who took two weeks to adjust to any adaptive change in their contact center. They supported vacation properties across many locations in the United States. A change in local regulations or details about a partner organization would all have to go through the following process:

1. They would create a new course in the LMS.
2. They would gradually cycle agents off the phones over a two-week period to go through the training.

While the change was being rolled out, there were some agents who were working with the updated procedures and others who were working from outdated knowledge. It was inefficient, frustrating, and error-prone.

After they implemented digital guides, they moved to the Train Stage. They were able to cut the time to change down to almost nothing.

Each morning, agents would receive a list of important procedures that had been updated. Since they were trained to follow the digital guides every time they handled a call, they just needed to pay attention to the changes in the updated guides.

This agility became even more important when COVID hit. State and local policies were changing on a minute-by-minute basis. Can you imagine if they had still been taking two weeks to roll out changes in the contact center? Instead, they were able to instantly adapt to each regulation change and give their customers accurate and timely guidance.

Transformational Change

Transformational change is much more involved. The role of knowledge operations in transformational change is to decrease the productivity dip in the J-Curve.

The J-Curve measures the relative productivity of an organization before, during, and after a transformational change.

Before the change, the organization has a base level of performance. As the change is introduced, performance dips as employees have to unlearn old behaviors and learn and adopt new ones.

The hope is that, eventually, the organization will arrive at a new status quo where performance is higher than it was at the original state.

Because Guide, Train, and Accelerate organizations are able to adjust to changes so quickly, they spend less time operating at the bottom of the J-Curve.

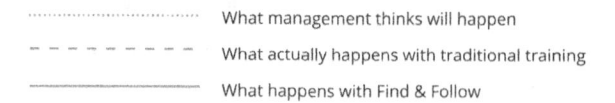

Find & Follow

.... What management thinks will happen
– – – – – What actually happens with traditional training
———— What happens with Find & Follow

What People Think Will Happen

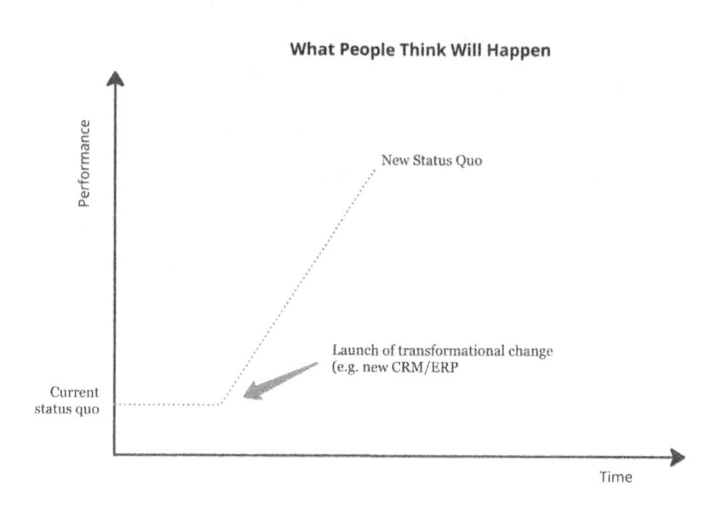

Performance vs *Time*

New Status Quo

Launch of transformational change (e.g. new CRM/ERP)

Current status quo

What Actually Happens With Traditional Training

Performance vs *Time*

Launch of transformational change (e.g. new CRM/ERP)

Current status quo

Performance improvements take much longer to achieve than anticipated

Performance decrease (bottom of the J-curve)

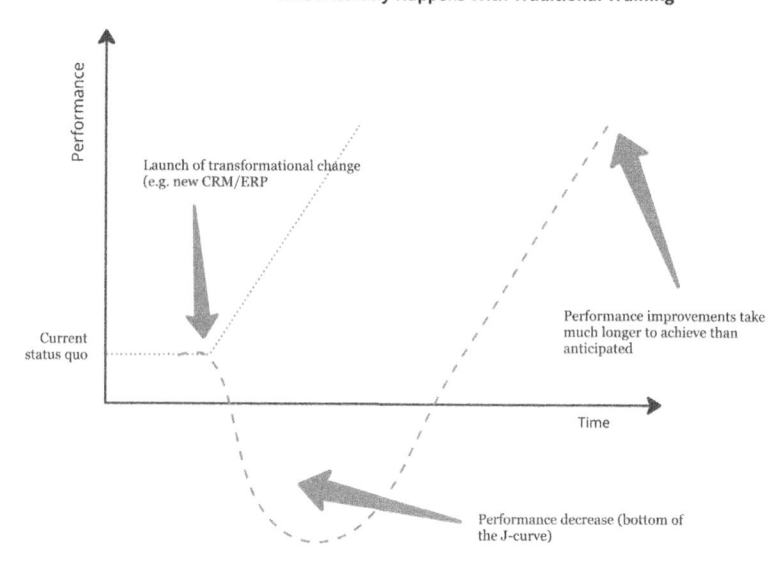

The Benefits of Moving Up the Knowledge Ops Maturity Model

We had one customer that was rolling out a new CRM for the third time after two previous failed attempts. For this rollout, they moved to the Train Stage.

All that was required was two days of training on how to use the digital guides. On launch day, they had 99% adoption and almost zero support requests. As tweaks were made to the CRM post-launch, guides were updated, and employees instantly adapted. They spent almost no time at the bottom of the J-Curve.

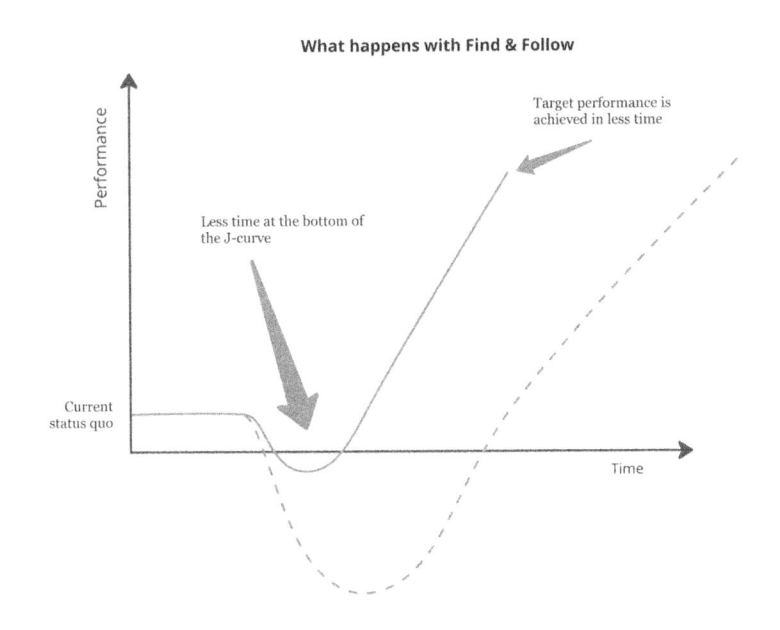

What happens with Find & Follow

A graph with Performance on the y-axis and Time on the x-axis. Annotations indicate "Less time at the bottom of the J-curve," "Target performance is achieved in less time," and "Current status quo."

> **Summary**
>
> Organizations that operate at the Guide, Train, or Accelerate stages will see the following:
> - Significant cost savings around employee onboarding times and staffing requirements
> - An improved culture of less stress, more confidence, and greater accountability
> - An improved ability to adjust to both adaptive and transformational changes in the organization

The benefits of moving up the Knowledge Ops Maturity Model are significant. But how do we do it?

That is where the Find & Follow Framework comes in, and that is what we will tackle in the next section.

Part III:

The Find & Follow Framework

"The only thing that you absolutely have to know is the location of the library."
– Albert Einstein

Chapter 5:

Three Core Beliefs of the Find & Follow Framework

In this chapter, you will:

- Learn the three core beliefs behind the Find & Follow Framework
- Be introduced to the Knowledge Operations Flywheel

Find & Follow is a framework that allows you to move up to the higher stages of the Knowledge Ops Maturity Model. It is a toolset for helping you move out of the quicksand of tribal knowledge and onto the smooth highway of rapid knowledge transfer.

You accomplish this by enabling your employees to rely less on memorization or tribal knowledge and more on just-in-time guidance that is findable and followable in the context they work in.

The framework is based on three core beliefs:

1. We can do more by memorizing less.
2. We can learn while we do.
3. We can clarify complexity.

Belief 1: We Can Do More by Memorizing Less

Your working memory is a temporary storage space where you hold and use information to do things like solve a problem, make a decision, or complete a complex task. But it has limits. When you have to overload your working memory in order to do your job, you experience more stress and more fatigue, and you are more likely to make mistakes.

In his book *Effortless*, author Greg McKeown describes the limits of working memory:

> *The limits of working memory breed avoidable errors. Extreme complexity only increases the cognitive load, making us that much more prone to errors. So what we need is not more knowledge but new skills and strategies that allow us to apply that knowledge without taxing our working memory.*[6]

My oldest son has cerebral palsy and is not able to ride a bike on his own. To help him have more experience with the outdoors, we purchased a bike trailer. He would sit in the back while I did my best to peddle him around. He had a great time, and I got a very good workout, especially when climbing hills. With even a gentle slope, I could really feel the difference when I was pulling his trailer behind me. As he got older (and bigger), the impact of his increased weight outpaced my ability to keep up physically, and I wasn't able to peddle him up those hills anymore.

But what if we had had an electric trailer? It didn't necessarily need to propel me forward. But if it could offer just enough

---

[6] Greg McKeown, *Effortless: Make it Easier to Do What Matters Most.* Random House, Kindle Edition p. 176

propulsion to offset the added weight of my son, I would have been able to take him almost anywhere.

Our minds work very much the same way as my bike did with my son's trailer attached. When we increase the cognitive load by requiring employees to complete long or complex tasks from memory, we make performance very, very difficult. When their minds become overloaded, they experience increased stress, frustration, and fatigue. At the same time, their task time and error rates increase.

Some information needs to be memorized and internalized by employees. But most operational information does not. By offloading the amount of information an employee needs to keep in their mind, we essentially allow the employee to peddle up a steep hill without feeling the additional weight of a trailer behind them.

We like to think of Find & Follow as reducing "cognitive weight." The more information that can be stored (and used) in a checklist, decision tree, or article, the less cognitive weight the employee has to carry.

Belief 2: We Can Learn While We Do

This is a hard one for trainers to accept, but the truth is that we can teach more by saying less and letting the learners do more. Trainers often believe that they need to cover everything in their training. But we all know that just because you covered something in training doesn't mean that an employee will be able to recall and use that information when they need it.

Employees will learn faster if they encounter challenges, create questions in their minds, and then discover the answers that they can easily follow on their own.

Former Harvard Business School Professor and author Clayton Christensen has said, "Questions are places in your mind where answers fit. If you haven't asked the question, the answer has nowhere to go."[7]

We love to use cooking analogies.

Imagine two groups of people learning to bake bread. One group spends 60 minutes listening to a lecture with 80 PowerPoint slides.

The second group hears a brief explanation of some key concepts, is given a recipe, and then actually bakes some bread.

A week later, which group would be better prepared to successfully bake bread on their own? Clearly, the second group—especially if they were able to use the same recipe again.

By lecturing less and providing more opportunities for employees to practice finding and following our digital guides (our recipe books), our employees will learn more in less time.

Belief 3: We Can Clarify the Complex

Sometimes CEOs or VPs say, "Well, we just need to make things simpler." An operations director hears this and thinks, "Buy me a magic wand, and I will make it so."

Removing complexity from a process is never easy and, in some cases, impossible, given the available resources.

But even if we can't simplify a process, we *can* clarify it.

I used to live in Boston during the "Big Dig." It was a huge construction project that took much more time and money than anyone had anticipated. To make matters worse, it was all happening right by the tunnel we needed to take to the airport.

Each time I went to the airport to pick someone up, it seemed that the route had changed because of the construction. This

---

[7] https://twitter.com/claychristensen/status/231411154050748416?lang=en

was before the time of the ubiquitous GPS unit in your phone, so I would have to pay close attention to the various detour signs to make sure I didn't end up just making another loop around Faneuil Hall.

The turn-by-turn directions to get to the airport were complex, and I often made mistakes.

Fast forward to today. Would that be a problem? Probably not. Now I have a GPS unit. Even if there were just as many turns and detours as there were back in the 90s, I would be able to navigate them easily. My GPS unit makes it simple to follow complex directions. The GPS doesn't remove the complexity of the directions. It just clarifies what I need to do.

By clarifying complexity, we can reduce the errors, training time, and mental strain associated with even your most complex procedures.

These three beliefs, (1) that we can do more by remembering less, (2) that we can teach more by speaking less, and (3) that we can clarify complexity, form the foundation of the Find & Follow Framework.

What Do We Want to Achieve With Find & Follow?

Our end goal with Find & Follow is to transfer knowledge as efficiently as possible. When it comes to transferring actionable knowledge for performing operational tasks, we believe that providing employees with digital guides that are easy to find and follow (hence the name) is the best approach.

When employees have digital guides that efficiently transfer knowledge to them as they perform a task, you begin to pick up momentum. The graphic below shows the overall process a Find & Follow Organization follows. It is called the Knowledge Ops

Flywheel and represents what happens when you can transfer knowledge instantly.

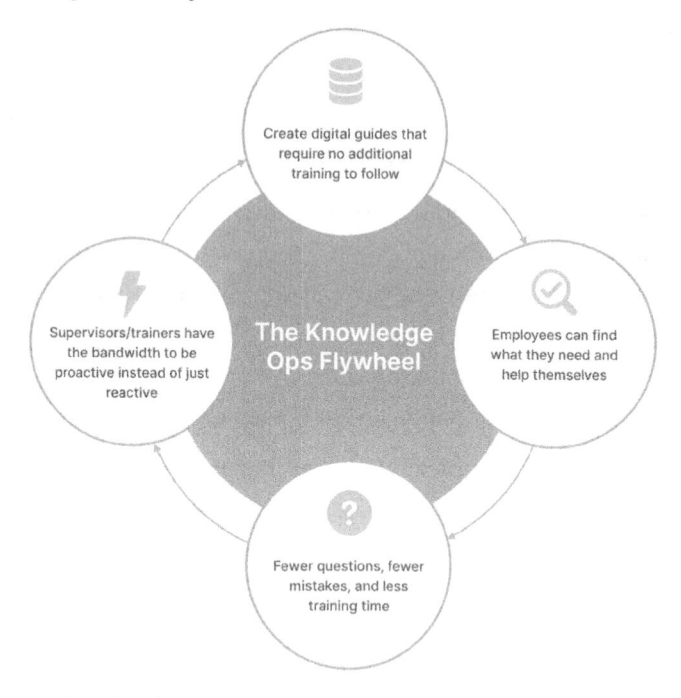

Diagram: The Knowledge Ops Flywheel

- Create digital guides that require no additional training to follow
- Employees can find what they need and help themselves
- Fewer questions, fewer mistakes, and less training time
- Supervisors/trainers have the bandwidth to be proactive instead of just reactive

You can download a PDF of this graphic at www.screensteps.com/find-follow-book/resources

A flywheel is a concept in business originally introduced by Jim Collins in his book *Good to Great: Why Some Companies Make the Leap ... and Others Don't*. It represents a process that gains momentum as it moves forward, continually improves, and has a compounding effect on your organization.

The Knowledge Ops Flywheel shows how your organization will become more and more productive as you create digital guides that can transfer knowledge immediately.

It has four parts:

1. Create digital guides that require no additional intervention to follow.

Three Core Beliefs of the Find & Follow Framework

2. Employees can find what they need and help themselves.
3. Fewer questions, fewer mistakes, and less training time.
4. Supervisors and trainers can be proactive instead of just reactive.

As more and more digital guides are created that can stand alone, the organization becomes more and more efficient, creating the flywheel effect.

Chapter 6:

The Four Systems

In this chapter, you will be introduced to:

- The four systems used in the Find & Follow Framework—Prepare, Train, Empower, and Adapt

At this point, I will only present a high-level overview of the systems. In Part IV of this book, you will learn detailed information about how to incorporate each system. For right now, we will just look at the systems from a 10,000-foot view.

The Find & Follow Framework will help you achieve this flywheel effect so that your team can:

- Onboard new hires in less time
- Get consistent performance no matter how complex things are
- Build confidence and work independently
- Respond to change no matter how big or small

It does this by giving you four systems to follow in your training and operations. Those four systems are called:

1. Prepare
2. Train
3. Empower
4. Adapt

The Four Systems of Find & Follow

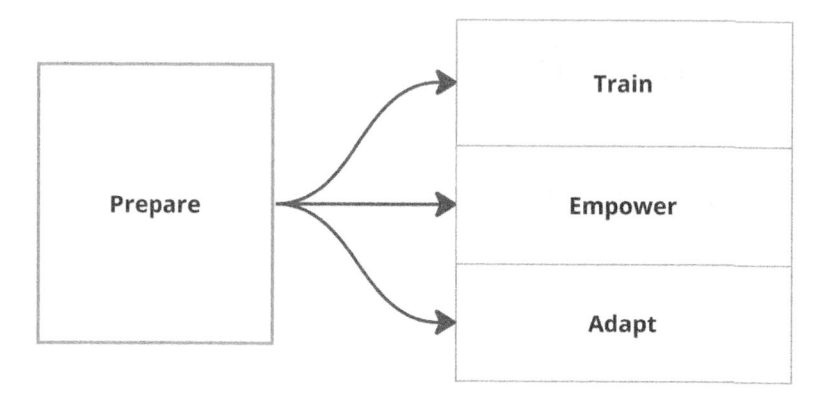

```
                    ┌─────────────┐
               ┌───►│    Train    │
┌──────────┐   │    ├─────────────┤
│ Prepare  │◄──┼───►│   Empower   │
└──────────┘   │    ├─────────────┤
               └───►│    Adapt    │
                    └─────────────┘
```

You can download a PDF of this graphic at screensteps.com/find-follow-book/resources

Prepare

The Prepare System guides your team in preparing the right digital guides in the right way. The goal is to design digital guides so that employees can quickly find them in an online knowledge base (almost like your own internal Google) and follow them. These digital guides provide the foundation for the other three systems and are used extensively in each.

Train

The Train System helps your team train new employees, cross-train employees, or train existing employees when major changes are introduced to the business. Training utilizes the guides you created in the Prepare System coupled with foundational courses and practice activities.

Empower

The Empower System helps your supervisors and managers empower your employees to perform efficiently and independently because they rely on the digital guides as they perform day-to-day operational tasks. This system helps the culture around how employees use digital guides to do their work.

Adapt

The Adapt System allows your team to effortlessly adapt to small changes and confidently adjust to major changes such as a new CRM/ERP, merger/acquisition, or any other transformative change.

Below is an outline of the components of each system.

Prepare
- Align + Define
- Design + Refine

Train
- Break Up the Topics
- Prepare Foundational Courses
- Prepare Practice Activities
- Run the Training Sessions

Empower
- Rely on the Digital Guides
- Redirect Questions
- Invest in Reusable Knowledge

Adapt
- Analyze the Impact
- Prepare the Guides
- Notify or Train

```
                                    Train
                            Break up the topics
                         Prepare Foundational Courses
                         Prepare Practice Activities
                          Run the Training Sessions

                                   Empower
      Prepare                Rely on the digital guides
   Align + Define                Redirect questions
   Design + Refine         Invest in reusable knowledge

                                    Adapt
                             Analyze the impact
                             Prepare the guides
                               Notify or train
```

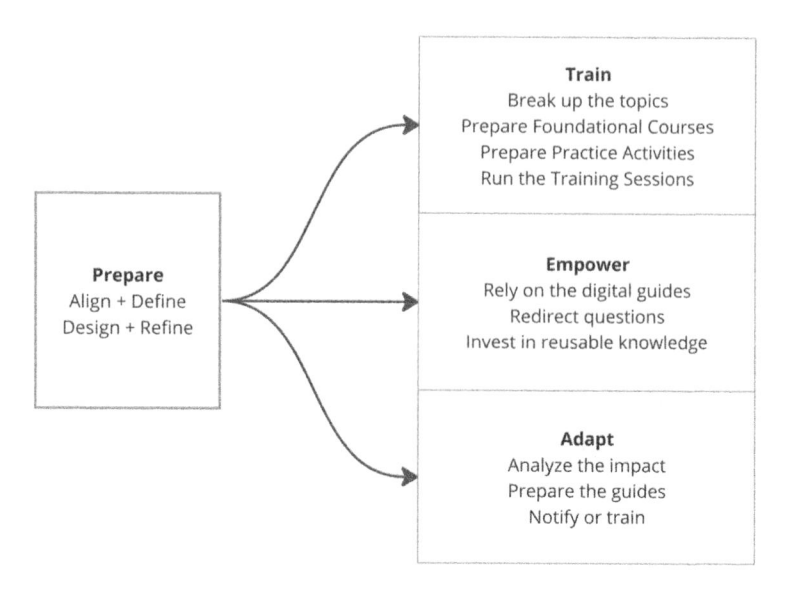

I'll introduce these concepts below. We will go into greater detail about how to implement these systems in later chapters.

System 1: Prepare

In order to see the kinds of transformations you read about earlier, you need to build a foundation of digital guides that can immediately transfer knowledge to employees. But creating digital guides isn't as simple as just sitting down and performing a knowledge dump. Those kinds of guides look like encyclopedias. What we're trying to create are easy-to-follow recipes.

So proper preparation is key.

We break the Prepare System into two parts:

1. Align + Define
2. Design + Refine

Align + Define

Have you ever heard a supervisor complain that your company's trainers aren't teaching employees the right skills? Have you ever heard trainers complain that the operations team isn't telling them about important changes in work requirements?

Align + Define solves that problem. One of the challenges of tribal knowledge is that it's not clear what people are supposed to do or how they're supposed to do it. That's why things feel so chaotic when onboarding new employees or making big changes to operations.

We need to get everyone on the same page so that things are clear and consistent.

When you complete the Align + Define process, your training, operations, and QA teams will have a crystal-clear understanding and a perfectly aligned agreement of exactly what skills and information an employee will need to work independently.

This all happens in what we call a Find & Follow Workshop. The output of that workshop will represent all the knowledge that needs to be transferred to an employee.

Design + Refine

Next, you need to prepare the digital guides. The Design + Refine process helps you create digital guides that employees can find, follow, and use in the moment they need them.

The digital guides you create are never perfect the first time you design them, so this process involves iterating very quickly—refining them—until employees can use them successfully.

We call this making your digital guides findable, followable, and scannable.

Not only will this provide clarity to your employees, but it will get everyone on the same page and doing things consistently.

Now, when you design and refine, you aren't just dumping knowledge onto a page. You are designing and refining information so that knowledge can be transferred instantly. The Design + Refine process will give you the guidance you need to create digital guides that are clear and effective.

System 2: Train

Find & Follow does away with long lectures, recorded webinars, and death by PowerPoint. In Find & Follow, your employees aren't required to memorize thousands of clicks and steps. They only memorize the necessary foundational knowledge, and then employees learn to follow digital guides for everything else.

The Train System consists of four parts:

1. Break Up the Topics
2. Prepare Foundational Courses
3. Prepare Practice Activities
4. Run the Training

Break Up the Topics

Our brains are like stomachs—they can only digest so much at a time. While it's common to dump everything out at once and say, "Bon appetit," that's not what we do in a Find & Follow Training.

Think of all the information that your new employees have to consume as a multi-course meal. Break things up into smaller chunks.

Prepare Foundational Courses

For each topic, you will prepare short foundational courses. Foundational courses aren't hour-long lectures. Foundational courses just teach key concepts that will help employees successfully follow the digital guides.

Think of these courses as explaining the "what," "why," "when," "where," and a high-level "how."

Prepare Practice Activities

Employees learn most by doing. You will prepare practice activities for each topic area that will allow your employees to practice using the digital guides to complete real-world tasks.

This is where your employees get into the more granular "how "of doing a task.

Run the Training Sessions

Once everything is prepared, it is time to run the training sessions. As you run the training, you will complete the following sequence of activities for each topic area:

- Lay the Foundation: You will present the foundational materials in a discussion or course. This will take 10–20% of the total training time.
- Introduce the Tools: You will give them a few minutes to become familiar with finding and following the digital guides.
- Practice the Activities: You will give your employees real-world scenarios that they will complete by using the digital guides. This is where you will spend 80–90% of your training time.

When you follow the Train System, you will cut your time to proficiency for employees by at least 50%. It's not that they're able to memorize more in less time—it's that employees will have to memorize less and be able to do more. As long as they can absorb the foundational information, they'll know enough to pull up a digital guide to respond to any request.

System 3: Empower

The Empower System enables your employees to work independently after they leave training. It consists of three steps:
1. Rely on the Digital Guides
2. Redirect Questions
3. Invest in Reusable Knowledge

Rely on the Digital Guides

Employees rely on the digital guides to do their work just like a cook relies on recipes to make meals. Many will believe that they will look more impressive if they can work without relying on the digital guides. But as soon as they start working from memorized information, you will see more mistakes and poorer performance.

This process will help your supervisors and managers motivate employees and hold them accountable for relying on the digital guides.

Redirect Questions

Employees will still come to supervisors, coaches, and managers with questions that are answered in your digital guides. Find & Follow Organizations need to resist the temptation to provide lengthy responses to those questions in a Slack/Teams message or email.

The Empower System teaches your supervisors, coaches, and managers how to redirect employees back to the digital guides in a helpful and encouraging way.

Invest in Reusable Knowledge

Inevitably questions or situations will come up that are not addressed in your digital guides. But Find & Follow Organizations are knowledge investors, not spenders.

The Empower System will teach your team how to invest in capturing knowledge instead of just spending all their time answering the same questions over and over again.

As you follow these three steps, you will empower your employees to work more efficiently and independently, and you will greatly reduce the time supervisors spend answering questions and fixing mistakes.

System 4: Adapt

The Adapt System will help you adapt to the regular changes that happen in an organization in less time and with less confusion. Some examples would be:

- A software update
- A change in procedure
- A temporary office closing
- A policy or regulation change

The Adapt System consists of three steps:

1. Analyze the Impact
2. Prepare the Guides
3. Notify or Train

Analyze the Impact

Your team will learn to analyze what impact the change will have on their team, determining which digital guides need to be updated and what, if any, additional foundational knowledge will need to be taught.

Prepare the Guides

After your team has understood the impact of the change, they will update the digital guides, ensuring that the new procedures are followable and scannable.

Notify or Train

In Find & Follow, not every change will require a new training session. Lunch and learns or training classes are used as a last resort and only when additional foundational knowledge is required or when practice activities may be necessary. The Notify or Train process will help your team decide if training and practice activities are required or if a simple notification will suffice.

Chapter 7:

What You Need for Find & Follow

In this chapter, you will learn:

- What resources you will need to have in place to successfully implement Find & Follow

To successfully implement Find & Follow, you will need three things:

1. Executive sponsorship
2. A team to implement it
3. A knowledge base with some additional features or a knowledge ops platform

Executive Sponsorship

Executive sponsorship is key to achieving success with Find & Follow. We have seen organizations where the L&D department has tried to apply Find & Follow principles without getting full executive sponsorship, and it never works out well.

Why? What usually happens is that the L&D team creates digital guides, but because they are not on the front lines, the digital guides don't match exactly what employees need to do.

L&D then asks supervisors and SMEs to contribute to the digital guides, but they are too busy answering questions and putting out fires to spend time writing something that they don't think any of their team members will ever use.

Find & Follow is a new way of working, and it will require an executive team that will sponsor the initiative, communicate the vision, align training and operations, and support the change.

A Team to Implement It

One person can't implement Find & Follow alone. You are going to need coordination between trainers, coaches, supervisors, and frontline employees.

- Trainers and supervisors will need to work closely together to gain alignment on what employees actually need to be able to do (the Prepare System helps ensure this happens).
- Trainers are going to have to lecture less and provide more practice opportunities (the Train System will help them make that shift).
- Supervisors and coaches are going to need to point frontline employees to digital guides (the Empower System will help them reinforce these new behaviors).

The point is the whole team needs to be involved. Find & Follow isn't something a trainer or supervisor can implement all by themselves.

A Knowledge Base (or a Knowledge Ops Platform)

Finally, you will need a knowledge base with some specific features. In our business, we call this a knowledge ops platform since it can be so different than a traditional knowledge base. A traditional knowledge base is going to focus on capturing, cataloging, and delivering knowledge.

What You Need for Find & Follow

A knowledge ops platform will do all of this but adds some additional capabilities that allow you to operationalize your organizational knowledge, not just capture it.

The most important capability is the ability to design digital guides that:

1. Can meet the needs of both new and experienced employees
2. Are findable and followable

It isn't enough to just have Word, PDF, or even online articles. The digital guides have to be designed to be followed correctly in high-stress situations and without slowing the employee down.

To accomplish this, the knowledge base or knowledge ops platform should be able to support standard articles, interactive checklists, and decision trees. We will explain this in detail in later chapters.

Our company, ScreenSteps, creates an online knowledge ops platform that incorporates all the capabilities required to support the Find & Follow Framework. You can learn more about it at www.screensteps.com.

Summary

- Find & Follow is a framework for moving up to stages 3 through 5 of the Knowledge Ops Maturity Model.
- The goal is to create an environment that transfers knowledge immediately by using digital guides that employees can find and follow without relying on memorized knowledge.
- Find & Follow consists of four systems to help you achieve this: Prepare, Train, Empower, and Adapt.
- To implement the four systems, you will need executive sponsorship, a team to implement Find & Follow, and a knowledge ops platform.

I will explain each of these systems in detail in Part IV of this book. But now that we understand the key parts of the framework let's describe how your team will feel different once you implement Find & Follow.

Chapter 8:

How Will Find & Follow Be Different Than What You Are Doing Now?

In this chapter, you will learn how Find & Follow will impact different roles in your organization, including:

- New hires
- Tier 2 support reps
- Supervisors
- Trainers
- Content authors
- Senior management

If you have never worked in a Find & Follow Organization, it can be hard to imagine what it is like. In this chapter, we are going to help clarify those differences by letting you experience different roles in your organization and how Find & Follow will impact them.

New Hires

Imagine that you have just been hired into the loan operations department of a regional-sized bank. You are expecting to go through several weeks of training and then several more of shadowing, just like you have in every other company you have worked in.

But this place is different. On the second day, your instructor spends 20 minutes explaining the key concepts behind loan processing. After the short lecture, you are introduced to the knowledge base you will be using. You spend a few minutes clicking around the knowledge base, getting familiar with how it is laid out and the different ways you can interact with the digital guides.

Before you have a chance to get bored, the instructor asks you to go through some practice activities. You have never been trained to handle the scenarios she throws at you, but the instructor assures you that if you find and follow the right digital guides, you will be able to handle each scenario successfully.

You dive in. At first, you feel unsure of yourself and unsure of the digital guides. Your instructor doesn't correct your mistakes. She just encourages you to refer back to the digital guide when you make an error.

The digital guides are different than what you have seen in other places where you have worked. There are no giant walls of text or massive PowerPoint files.

Instructions are presented as checklists, short reference articles, or decision trees that give you instructions one step at a time. Important parts of the instructions are clearly called out. The guides are very easy to scan while you are working.

After practicing a few scenarios, you start to gain confidence. You realize that by using the digital guides, you can handle almost any scenario that is thrown at you.

How Will Find & Follow Be Different Than What You Are Doing Now?

For the next few days, your training follows the same pattern. You spend about 20–30 minutes on a new topic and then several hours going through practice activities around that topic.

After four days, you are ready to start taking on real tasks. You never do any shadowing. You use the same digital guides in your day-to-day work that you did in training. This is the most capable and confident you have felt in any job you have ever had.

Tier 2 Support Engineer

Now imagine that you are a Tier 2 support engineer. You spend all your time handling escalations and solving complex problems. There aren't a lot of people with your level of expertise, so you end up having to work a lot of overtime. It's exhausting.

But several months ago, your team adopted Find & Follow, and now your supervisor is asking you to create digital guides that will eliminate some of the escalations you are receiving. You are doubtful this will work, but your supervisor informed you that management was behind the change and you needed to give it a shot.

So, you carve out some time to sit down with Karen from training. You have identified two scenarios to address. Karen talks you through how you would troubleshoot those issues, building out a decision tree as you speak.

The first draft isn't nearly complete. But it does give you a starting point. As you remember more and more variables and edge cases, you add them to the decision tree.

Once you feel it is ready, you try it out with a Tier 1 agent. They do OK, but you notice some areas where they get stuck or confused. You make some quick improvements and have them try again.

Success!

You roll the decision tree out to all the agents. All of a sudden, escalations around that topic start to drop. And even when an escalation comes through, a lot of the standard troubleshooting has already been completed, allowing you to identify the problem more quickly.

Work becomes a better place to be. Your backlog is down. You don't feel as stressed. You are now looking to build additional decision trees that Tier 1 agents can use to solve cases without escalating them to you.

Supervisors

Next, let's imagine the role of a supervisor. Before implementing Find & Follow, you spent a lot of time helping out with tasks and answering questions. You really didn't feel like you were supervising much. You were too busy doing everyone else's job.

But since you implemented Find & Follow, things have changed. Employees don't have nearly as many questions as they did before.

You have had to break some long-held habits. You used to answer questions right away in Microsoft Teams or hop on a video call to walk someone through a procedure. Now you point them to the knowledge base or take some time to build a digital guide that answers their question.

Your employees now know to turn to the knowledge base first before asking for help. This has really increased their independence and their confidence.

You spend more time creating and updating digital guides than you used to, but you realize that you now have more mental bandwidth and time to focus on improving your team since you aren't answering so many questions and fixing so many mistakes.

Trainers

Each new hire's training used to be so stressful. You had to work so hard to keep people engaged. And then supervisors would complain that you hadn't trained the new hires well enough.

It wasn't uncommon to finish training a new group only to find out that some of the procedures you had taught them were out of date. It all seemed like such a waste of time and energy.

Now, with Find & Follow, you and the supervisors are on the same page. You use the exact same digital guides in training that supervisors provide to their team, so there is no risk of your training getting out of sync with operations.

And new-hire training sessions are a breeze. Your foundational courses and practice activities are all prepared. You don't have to worry about keeping people engaged. The practice activities do that for you. You have a repeatable training program that reliably produces employees who are ready to work independently.

Content Authors

As a content author, your job often felt pointless. You would spend hours creating documentation that never got used. You wondered if anyone valued what you did at all.

All that has changed after implementing Find & Follow. People are using the guides all the time and constantly offering feedback on how they can be improved.

You have had to learn to publish faster and make small changes as needed. You used to take days or weeks to prepare documentation. But now that employees rely on the guides to do their work, you often have to publish changes in a matter of minutes and hours, not days or weeks.

You have had to learn to write a bit differently. You used to focus on just making sure everything was complete. Now you focus on ensuring employees can easily follow the guides you create.

It is certainly a different pace than you have been used to, but the knowledge operations software has tools to help you keep up.

You now feel like you are an important part of the business and can clearly see how your work impacts everyone on the team.

Senior Management

So much is different now that you have implemented Find & Follow. You used to have zero transparency into the operations of each department, but now all their procedures are clear to see. You even feel like you could handle a support call successfully.

Considering any sort of major change used to seem overwhelming. But you have seen how Find & Follow has made your employees more agile. Last month, you changed a major internal process, and your employees adapted almost immediately.

Training employees on the new process was a breeze, and the change cut the task time by 50%.

You now feel like you can adopt new technologies or processes without the struggle and loss in productivity that you always experienced before adopting Find & Follow.

You are seeing a level of consistency and efficiency that you really didn't think was possible.

How Will Find & Follow Be Different Than What You Are Doing Now?

> **Summary**
> Find & Follow will change key aspects of your work environment, including:
> - How employees are trained
> - How higher-skilled employees leverage their knowledge and time
> - How supervisors support employees
> - How trainers build training programs
> - How content writers create and prepare content
> - How senior management considers change initiatives

In the next section, we are going to dive into implementing Find & Follow for your team.

PART IV:

Implementing the Find & Follow Framework in Your Business

"We may be very busy, we may be very efficient, but we will also be truly effective only when we begin with the end in mind."
– Stephen Covey

Chapter 9:

Build Your Knowledge Ops Team

In this chapter, you will learn:

- What a knowledge ops team is
- Who needs to be on it
- What the responsibilities of a Knowledge Champion are
- How a Find & Follow Coach can help you implement Find & Follow
- The importance of communicating exactly what Find & Follow will look like to your entire team

As we mentioned before, you are going to need a team to implement Find & Follow. We like to call this your Knowledge Operations Team. They are the group of people that will be in charge of transferring knowledge to employees as efficiently as possible.

Who Is on the Team?

The team needs to consist of the following:

- Anyone in charge of training or coaching employees
- Anyone in charge of answering employee questions and fixing their mistakes

- Ideally, someone who has experience in the role or roles you are supporting

In practice, this usually consists of at least a trainer, supervisor, and senior frontline employee.

Other team members might include:

- QA experts
- Subject matter experts
- Compliance officers
- Documentation specialists

These team members will:

- Participate in the Find & Follow Workshop
- Work together to prepare, test, and approve digital guides

The Knowledge Champion

Someone on the team will need to be designated as the Knowledge Champion. The Knowledge Champion takes ownership of ensuring that guides are findable, followable, and scannable. They enable everyone to be more consistent and efficient.

In most situations, the Knowledge Champion is either a senior employee or a trainer who has a lot of experience in operations.

Find & Follow Coaches

If this is your first time implementing Find & Follow, you can also benefit from the assistance of a coach. Find & Follow coaches will help you:

- Facilitate Find & Follow Workshops
- Separate out foundational and actionable knowledge
- Prepare digital guides
- Prepare and run Find & Follow Training sessions

If you would like the assistance of a Find & Follow coach, then get in touch with the authors. We would be happy to help you out.

Make Sure Everyone Is on the Same Page

Before you begin, you need to make sure everyone on the team understands what you are trying to accomplish.

Ideally, they would all read this book. But at the very least, you should help them understand these two diagrams:

- The Knowledge Ops Maturity Model
- The Knowledge Ops Flywheel

The Knowledge Ops Maturity Model

	Stage 5: Accelerate
We want to be here	Stage 4: Train
	Stage 3: Guide
	Stage 2: Document
We are here	Stage 1: Tribal

⟶ Employee Independence ⟶

Find & Follow

The Knowledge Ops Flywheel

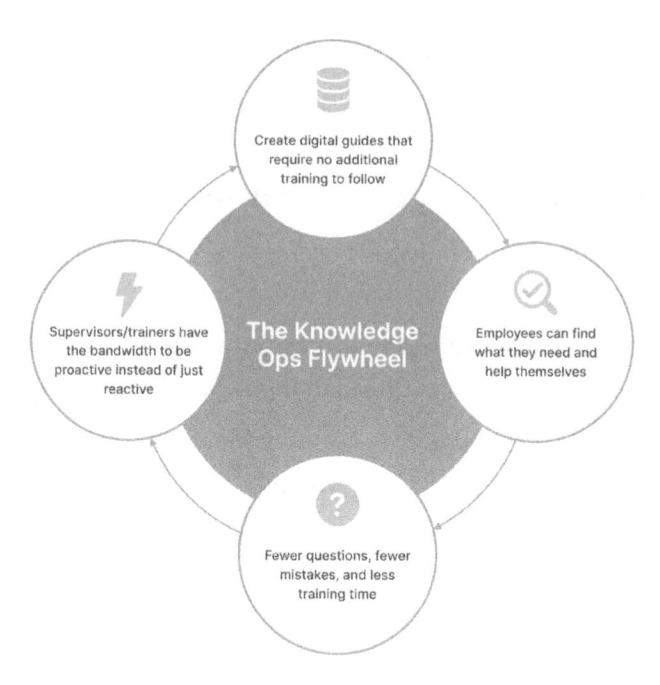

- Create digital guides that require no additional training to follow
- Employees can find what they need and help themselves
- Fewer questions, fewer mistakes, and less training time
- Supervisors/trainers have the bandwidth to be proactive instead of just reactive

These diagrams will help everyone understand what you are trying to accomplish:

- No more reliance on tribal knowledge
- Digital guides that can stand alone
- An organization that becomes more and more efficient

Summary

- Your knowledge ops team will consist of trainers, supervisors, QA experts, senior frontline, and others who are responsible for answering employee questions and fixing their mistakes.
- You will need to designate a Knowledge Champion who will be responsible for ensuring employees have digital guides to support them in their work.
- You will want to make sure that everyone on the team understands the vision of what you are trying to achieve by either sharing this book with them or discussing the Knowledge Ops Maturity Model and the Knowledge Ops Flywheel.

Now that we have assembled the team let's start implementing the four systems.

Chapter 10:

The Prepare System Part 1 – Align + Define

In this chapter, you will learn:

- The components of the first part of the Prepare System – Align + Define
- The importance of the Find & Follow Workshop
- How to run the workshop
- How to prepare the workshop report

As a reminder, there are four systems you will use to successfully implement Find & Follow. These are:

1. Prepare – This system will help you prepare the digital guides that employees will use during training and while performing their responsibilities.
2. Train – This system can be used to onboard new employees or implement a transformational change (e.g., a new CRM/ERP system) very quickly and effectively.
3. Empower – This system will be used to empower employees to work confidently and independently during their day-to-day work.
4. Adapt – This system will help your team adapt to the changes that any business experiences on a regular basis.

In this chapter, we will describe the first half of the Prepare System—Align + Define. We will cover the other systems in subsequent chapters.

The Prepare System

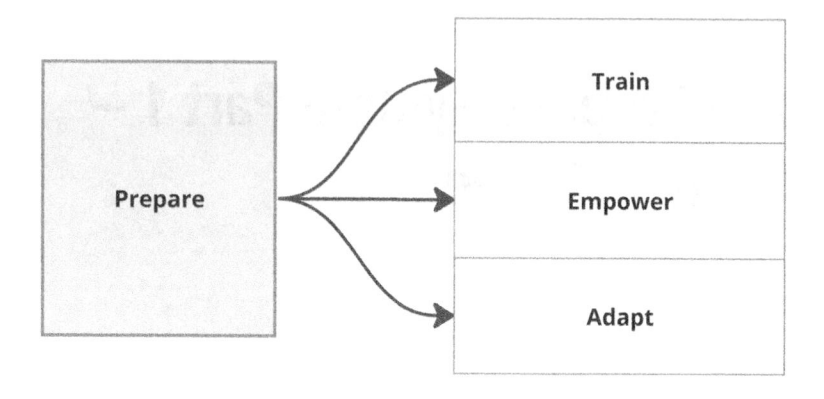

The Prepare System will help you ensure the following:

- You identify all of the digital guides that need to be created.
- You design guides that employees can find and follow without needing assistance.

To accomplish this, there are two parts to the Prepare System:

1. Align + Define
2. Design + Refine

Align + Define: The Find & Follow Workshop

Your employees can't work independently unless they have the right digital guides. And they can't have the right digital guides unless your training, coaching, and operational teams are completely aligned around what the employee needs to do and how they need to do it.

The Find & Follow Workshop is the mechanism for creating that alignment and defining those processes. In this section, we will explain:

1. Why you need a workshop
2. Who should attend
3. What the workshop will produce
4. How to run the workshop

> TIPS FROM THE TRENCHES
>
> Don't skip this step. The Find & Follow Workshop is crucial to a successful Find & Follow program. Most organizations don't really understand what their employees need to be able to do. The Find & Follow Workshop will help you clearly identify what employees need to know and do in order to be knowledgeable, consistent, and efficient.

Why a Workshop?

Often when we bring on a new customer, they tell us that they don't need a workshop. They are always wrong.

Our customers who engage in the Find & Follow Workshops launch their Find & Follow programs faster and with fewer mistakes.

Too often, supervisors and trainers think that they just need to create some simple guides, and employees will be able to do their jobs. The reality is that they haven't fully understood all that an employee needs to know to be able to work independently.

At this point, it can be helpful to revisit the Knowledge Ops Flywheel:

The Knowledge Ops Flywheel

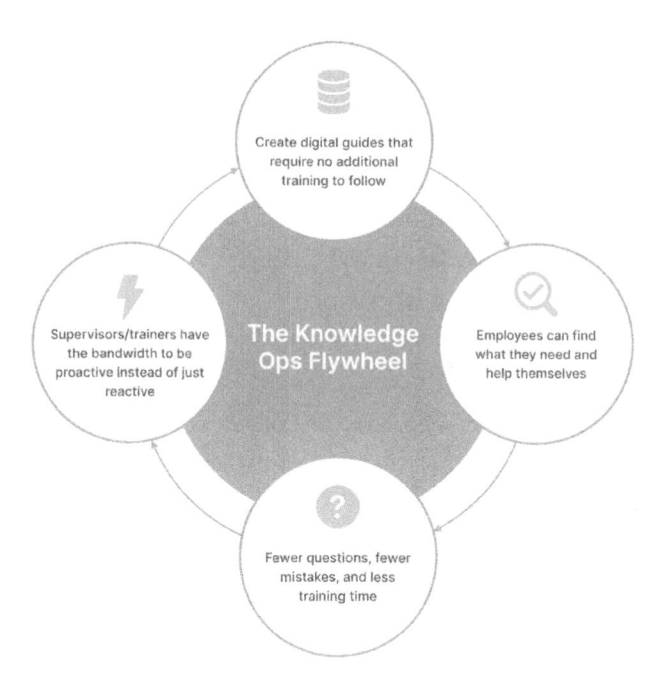

- Create digital guides that require no additional training to follow
- Employees can find what they need and help themselves
- Fewer questions, fewer mistakes, and less training time
- Supervisors/trainers have the bandwidth to be proactive instead of just reactive

Without a comprehensive workshop, we can't create all the guides employees will need to work independently.

The workshop will help us solve two problems:

1. The misalignment between training and operations
2. Digital guides that are incomplete or that can't stand alone

Problem 1: The Misalignment Between Training and Operations

Most organizations suffer from a misalignment between training and operations. The training department spends days, weeks, or months training new hires only to send them off to supervisors without the knowledge they need to perform basic tasks independently.

Supervisors complain that training isn't preparing people properly. Trainers complain that operations isn't giving them all of the information they need to adequately train new hires.

This misalignment creates frustration, confusion, and performance delays that cost businesses hundreds of thousands if not millions of dollars. It also creates burnout and stress for those supervisors who have to fill in the knowledge gaps (or craters) left by inadequate or incomplete training.

The Find & Follow Workshop creates perfect alignment between training and operations. Trainers understand exactly what operations needs employees to do. Operations can communicate clearly what knowledge will be required by their employees.

Problem 2: Most Documentation (or Digital Guides) Can't Stand Alone

The other problem is that most documentation is terribly incomplete. Since documentation has not been designed with performance in mind, crucial details are left out. These details around policy, procedure, or best practices are relegated to the tribal knowledge of the organization. They are things that everyone just needs to "know" somehow.

The documentation has not been designed to stand alone.

The Find & Follow Workshop fleshes out all the details that the digital guides will need to include—all the variables, problem situations, exceptions, and everything else that can make what seems like a simple task become very complex.

This isn't just a knowledge dump. It's an organized process for getting the full picture of all the knowledge that will need to be transferred to an employee for them to independently perform their job.

What Are the Results of a Find & Follow Workshop?

At the end of a Find & Follow Workshop, you should have a detailed report of the following:

- Tasks the employee will need to be able to perform
- Related sub-tasks
- Requests they will need to respond to
- Answers they will need to give
- Problems they will need to solve
- Decisions they will need to make

For the sake of simplicity, we will call these activities.

For each of these activities, you will also detail all the variables or exceptions that can impact that activity.

This report becomes the contract between training and operations.

Training says to operations, "If we prepare employees to perform all these activities independently, will that meet your needs?"

Operations sheds tears of joy and can hardly utter a word.

Who Attends?

If you don't have the right people in the workshop, then your results will be incomplete.

Each workshop should focus on one or a few closely related roles. Trying to cover too many roles in the same workshop will create confusion. It is better to run multiple workshops for each role than to try to tackle the responsibilities of all roles in a single workshop.

To make your list of workshop participants, first, clearly define the role the workshop will be discussing. Then make sure you have someone who can represent each of these perspectives:

- Someone responsible for answering employee questions
- Someone responsible for fixing their mistakes
- Someone responsible for training employees in the target role
- Ideally, someone with real-world experience working in the target role

You want to get all these people in the same room or in the same virtual meeting. It is not enough to interview them independently.

Why? Because they are going to disagree about how things are really done. It is better to hash out all these differences in opinion in real time instead of trying to reconcile conflicting responses later on.

You should plan at least 90 minutes to 3 hours for your initial meeting. You may need to schedule follow-up meetings as well.

Preparing the Report

The output of this workshop will be the Find & Follow Report. It will consist of five columns, as seen below. We will explain what goes in each column later on.

Topic Areas	Activities	Related Sub-Tasks	Variables	Concepts

Identifying Tasks, Requests, Problems, and Questions

During the workshop, you want to document all the tasks, requests, problems, and questions that this role will have to deal with. We call these **Activity Types**. It can be helpful to define a few terms.

- Tasks: These are the names of the actual tasks an employee performs, such as canceling an account or sending a quote.

- **Requests:** Anything someone else (customer, supervisor, or co-worker) asks the employee to do.
- **Problems:** Any problem the employee needs to solve. This could be troubleshooting something for themselves or someone else.
- **Questions:** Any questions the employee gets asked for which they need to provide an answer.

I'm sure you can think of some things that would fit into multiple Activity Types. Maybe you identify an activity that is both a Problem and a Request. That is fine. The purpose of the Activity Types is to identify all the activities, not to have each activity perfectly categorized.

Use Topic Areas to Help Identify Activities

When we first started doing this workshop, we would sit down with the client and ask them to identify the activities their employees needed to perform. They would come up with three or four and then start to struggle.

We found that having them identify topic areas first greatly improved the number of activities they could identify.

The topic areas you use will be specific to your business and the target job role. Here are some examples that you could use to generate your topic areas:

- Software applications that the employee will use
- Types of transactions they need to complete
- Reason codes that you use in your customer service software
- Customer segments that they will support

Once again, the purpose is not to have everything perfectly categorized. The purpose of the topic areas is to make sure you have identified as many activities as possible.

Here is an example of what our Topic Areas and Activities columns might look like if we were filling this report out for a bank.

Topic Areas	Activities	Related Sub-Tasks	Variables	Concepts
Mobile Banking	- Why isn't my deposit showing up? - Locked out of my app - Didn't get the access code - Can't make a deposit on phone			
ATM	- Card rejected - Can't process transactions - Remove restriction on card - Is my card locked?			
External Transfer	- Don't see external transfer account - Set up external transfer - How many can I link?			
Zelle				
Enrollment				
Check Verification				

Related Sub-Tasks

Now that we have identified the activities, we want to go a level deeper and capture the sub-tasks that relate to those activities. Let's look at the following scenario: A customer calls their bank and asks why a transaction is not showing up in their mobile banking app. To answer this question, the employee will need to perform some tasks:

Find & Follow

- Find the customer's account.
- Review transaction history.
- Ask questions about the missing transaction.
- Determine why the transaction is not appearing.

These tasks are really the building blocks that allow the employee to answer the customer's question. Capture these tasks in the "Related Tasks" column. See the example below.

Topic Areas	Activities	Related Sub-Tasks	Variables	Concepts
Mobile Banking	- Why isn't my deposit showing up? - Locked out of my app - Didn't get the access code - Can't make a deposit on phone	- Review trans. history - Send request - Resend code - Review for locks		
ATM	- Card rejected - Can't process transactions - Remove restriction on card Is my card locked?	- Review for locks - Send request - Review account		
External Transfer	- Don't see external transfer account - Set up external transfer - How many can I link?	- Review account - Set up procedure - Provide answer		
Zelle				
Enrollment				
Check Verification				

You don't need to go into detail about how to perform these tasks yet. You just want to make sure you get a general idea of what the tasks are and capture them.

Variables

Now that you have identified all your activities and related tasks, you need to go back and dig a little deeper into each one. Some tasks can seem simple on their surface but, in reality, become quite complex. Why? Because of variables that affect how the activity will be performed.

Let's look at an example of changing an account owner for a software application that an employee supports. The technical process of changing the account owner is probably very simple, but the policy around changing the account owner can be complex.

Variables you might identify that would impact this activity would be:

- Who is the support agent speaking to?
- Are they already a user in the application?
- Is the previous account owner available, or have they left the organization?
- Is there someone the support agent can contact to verify that they can make the change?

At this point, you don't need to document how each of these variables will affect the activity. You just need to identify which variables will need to be accounted for.

Below is our example report with the Variables column completed.

Find & Follow

Topic Areas	Activities	Related Sub-Tasks	Variables	Concepts
Mobile Banking	- Why isn't my deposit showing up? - Locked out of my app - Didn't get the access code - Can't make a deposit on phone	- Review trans. history - Send request - Resend code - Review for locks	- Deposited over weekend, flagged - Going to incorrect number - Outdated app	
ATM	- Card rejected - Can't process transactions - Remove restriction on card Is my card locked?	- Review for locks - Send request - Review account	- ATM out of order, card expired	
External Transfer	- Don't see external transfer account - Set up external transfer - How many can I link?	- Review account - Set up procedure - Provide answer	- Option not turned on	

Concepts

Finally, we need to capture the high-level concepts employees will need to understand to be able to complete the activities and perform the related tasks. Concepts are big-picture items such as:

- People: Who will they interact with? Different customer types, partners, internal teams, etc.
- High-level business processes: What does the business do? How do they fit into the big picture? For example, an employee at an insurance company may need to understand the high-level process of how a claim is processed.
- Industry-specific concepts: For example, a hospital employee working in billing may need to understand

The Prepare System Part 1 – Align + Define

concepts such as primary and secondary insurance, co-pays, etc.
- Software tools: What software will the employee have to use to do their job?

Below is our fully completed workshop report.

Topic Areas	Activities	Related Sub-Tasks	Variables	Concepts
Mobile Banking	- Why isn't my deposit showing up? - Locked out of my app - Didn't get the access code - Can't make a deposit on phone	- Review trans. history - Send request - Resend code - Review for locks	- Deposited over weekend, flagged - Going to incorrect number - Outdated app	- Mobile app - Banking lifecycle for mobile - Mobile limitations
ATM	- Card rejected - Can't process transactions - Remove restriction on card Is my card locked?	- Review for locks - Send request - Review account	- ATM out of order, card expired	- What is an ATM? - How does it work? - Lifecycle of an ATM - Limitations of an ATM
External Transfer	- Don't see external transfer account - Set up external transfer - How many can I link?	- Review account - Set up procedure - Provide answer	- Option not turned on	- What is an ext. transfer? - Lifecycle of ext. transfer - Why set up ext. transfer?

> **Summary**
>
> The Find & Follow Workshop will help you:
> - Align your training and operation teams
> - Identify the activities employees will need assistance in performing
> - Identify the concepts employees will need to understand in order to successfully use your digital guides
> - Identify the sub-tasks and variables that will impact your activities

Now that we have our report, we are ready for the next stage—Define & Refine.

Chapter 11:

The Prepare System Part 2 – Design + Refine

In this chapter, you will learn:

- The concepts behind the second part of the Prepare System—Design + Refine
- How to use the Find & Follow Workshop report to develop your digital guides
- How to break up your digital guides
- How to make your digital guides findable, followable, and scannable

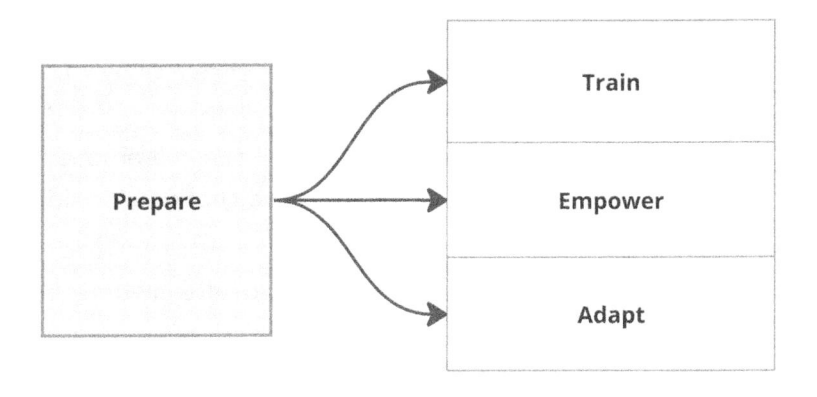

```
Prepare → Train
        → Empower
        → Adapt
```

The second part of the Prepare System is to Design + Refine. It is very important to understand a few key principles:

- We aren't going to just dump knowledge onto a page. We are going to design a guide that will help the employee perform correctly and efficiently.
- We aren't going to get everything right the first time. We are going to embrace a process of rapid iteration (or refinement) to get our guides to a state where they are performing effectively.

The Goal: Findable, Followable, and Scannable

Your goal should be to make every digital guide findable, followable, and scannable.

Findable means that an employee can find the guide they need in the moment when and in the context where they need it.

Followable means that the employee can follow the guide without making mistakes and without asking for assistance.

Scannable means that the guide is designed so that the employee can scan it and still follow it successfully. Many times, these guides need to be followed in high-pressure situations (e.g., while speaking to a customer or in an environment where there are many distractions). The more scannable you make your guides, the more successful they will be.

When we are evaluating digital guides that aren't producing the performance results the client wants, we check their guides against the following criteria:

- Is it findable? If not, then nothing else matters. An employee can't use what they can't find.
- Is it followable? If not, then we need to keep iterating on the guide until the employees can follow it successfully.

- Is it scannable? If not, we need to adjust the formatting and presentation so that important steps stand out.

The techniques described in this chapter will help you create digital guides that are findable, followable, and scannable.

Identifying Foundational Knowledge

One of the biggest challenges in designing digital guides that are findable, followable, and scannable is deciding what information you need to include and what information you can leave out.

The same problem happens when designing a training curriculum. How much do you need to cover? How do you strike that balance of being comprehensive without completely overwhelming the learner?

		Actionable Knowledge		*Foundational Knowledge*
Topic Areas	Activities	Related Sub-Tasks	Variables	Concepts
Mobile Banking	- Why isn't my deposit showing up? - Locked out of my app - Didn't get the access code - Can't make a deposit on phone	- Review trans. history - Send request - Resend code - Review for locks	- Deposited over weekend, flagged - Going to incorrect number - Outdated app	- Mobile app - Banking lifecycle for mobile - Mobile limitations
ATM	- Card rejected - Can't process transactions - Remove restriction on card - Is my card locked?	- Review for locks - Send request - Review account	- ATM out of order, card expired	- What is an ATM? - How does it work? - Lifecycle of an ATM - Limitations of an ATM

Find & Follow

External Transfer	- Don't see external transfer account - Set up external transfer - How many can I link?	-Review account - Set up procedure - Provide answer	- Option not turned on	- What is an ext. transfer? - Lifecycle of ext. transfer - Why set up ext. transfer?
Zelle				
Enrollment				
Check Verification				

Separating out foundational knowledge from actionable knowledge can simplify these decisions.

Actionable knowledge is any knowledge that needs to be used to complete the activities that you identified in the Find & Follow Workshop.

Foundational knowledge is any background information you would need to understand in order to successfully follow the guides. Foundational knowledge gives context to the employee. It helps them understand their surroundings, increasing their confidence and independence while following the digital guides.

The table below gives some examples for a banking institution.

Foundational Knowledge	Actionable Knowledge
• What type of customers do we work with?	• How do you create a new loan application?
• What software applications will you use?	• How old do you need to be to apply for a loan?
• How is money transferred between financial institutions? (high-level)	• How do I create a Wire Transfer request?
• How does a loan get approved and processed? (high-level)	• How do I apply a payment to a loan?

The important distinction is that actionable knowledge should never be memorized, while a basic understanding of foundational knowledge *should* be internalized by the employee.

Let's look at another example from a medical billing company.

Foundational Knowledge	Actionable Knowledge
• How does a medical bill get paid? (high-level) • What type of people will you be calling? • How do we work with insurance carriers? • What software applications will you use?	• How do I apply a payment? • How do I look up the payment history for a patient? • How do I issue a refund? • What do I do if the procedure was not covered by the insurance company?

Once you have separated out your foundational knowledge, you can create digital guides that either focus on the actionable knowledge or focus on the foundational knowledge. You can always link one to the other so that if an employee is reviewing a digital guide that explains the foundational knowledge and they need to then perform a related action, they can click the link and view the digital guide that walks them through the process.

And if an employee is viewing a digital guide for actionable knowledge and they need more foundational understanding, they can click the link to view the guide that provides more background information.

We can also address foundational knowledge within instructor-led or self-paced courses, which is handled by the Train System described in a later chapter.

Use the Report

Luckily, the Find & Follow Workshop Report has prepared us to easily separate foundational and actionable knowledge.

Everything that shows up in the Concept column will be foundational knowledge. Everything that is in the Related Tasks column is actionable knowledge.

Creating Actionable Digital Guides

The next step is to turn this wonderful Find & Follow Report into digital guides that can efficiently transfer operational knowledge.

In this section, we will cover:

- How to break up your digital guides
- How to make your guides findable, followable, and scannable

Breaking up Your Digital Guides

Now that you have separated the foundational and actionable knowledge, it is time to start breaking up the guides.

At this point, we want to really focus on the end result we need to achieve. We need a digital guide that an employee can find and follow without having to interrupt others for help and without making others (e.g., a customer or coworker) wait for them. Keeping that end goal in mind will help us know how to break up our guides.

> TIPS FROM THE TRENCHES
>
> BIG MISTAKE: We see many organizations that try to build one guide or manual to handle every activity or task. Their thought is, "This will be easier if I just put everything in the same document. That way, my employees just have one place to go to."
>
> It may sound good in theory, but in practice, it becomes a disaster. By putting everything into one massive document, you will make two things more difficult:
>
> - It will be harder for your team to maintain the content. Tracking the accuracy of a massive document is much more difficult than tracking the accuracy of individual guides targeted at specific activities.
> - It will be much harder for your employees to jump right to the guidance they need for the activity they are performing.
>
> When structuring articles, I like to compare the process to building a recipe book. I don't want to have one recipe that covers creating the whole meal. I should create separate recipes for each dish. Each recipe is its own article.

Step 1: Make It Findable

Many people believe that the key to helping employees find the information they need is to improve their search technology. But your search technology is probably only part of the problem.

Google has some of the best search technology in the world, but despite that, internet marketers build a career on designing content that can be found. You don't need to become an SEO master, but you do need to apply some simple principles that will make your content more findable.

Getting the Title Right

Most knowledge base articles have terrible titles. A good article title should help an employee know that they have found the right article *without* having to open the article.

> TIPS FROM THE TRENCHES
>
> We often hear that departments want to create an internal Google. Well, just as your web marketers have to follow search engine optimization best practices, you need to follow them too. Titles, readability, and scannability are all important aspects of making your content more findable.

For example, an employee may be looking for a guide about updating the billing address on a customer account. We have seen situations where this information was buried in an article titled "Billing" or "Addresses." Those aren't helpful titles.

A much better title would be "How to Update the Billing Address on a Customer Account" or "Updating the Billing Address for a Customer."

When an employee sees one of those titles, they will know right away that they have found the right article.

Another tip is to imagine what you would like to see if you were searching for help on Google. If you need help fixing a hole in your drywall, would you be more likely to click on an article titled "Drywall tips" or an article titled "How to Repair a Hole in Your Drywall"?

You should also avoid corporate jargon in your titles. Use the terms that your employees or customers are likely to use. We worked with one client who couldn't figure out why people weren't using their docs. We looked at their search reports and saw people searching for "theme customization." I asked if they had an article on theme customization. They said they did, but it was called "Branding." Renaming the article solved the problem.

Getting the title right will solve many of your findability problems.

Further Breaking Up Content

Sometimes the information an employee is looking for is in the middle of an existing guide. Maybe you have a guide that describes your procedure for processing returns. It may cover the responsibilities of several roles in your organization:

- The agent that sets up the RMA
- The warehouse staff that receives the return
- The QA team that inspects the return
- The finance team that refunds the purchase

When the QA team needs to find their instructions for inspecting the return, they find the directions buried halfway down in a large document where 75% of the material doesn't even apply to their role.

If this is the case, you need to back up and rethink how you are structuring things. Each digital guide should apply to a single role in your organization. The guide described above would be very useful for a manager who wants to see everything that the return process entails. But it is less useful for the individual roles that have to implement that process.

A better solution would be to break this up into four separate guides, one for each role in the organization. You could then create a fifth guide that gives an overview of the process, linking out to the role-specific guides.

A common technique for mapping out business processes is to use swim lanes (see the example below).

Find & Follow

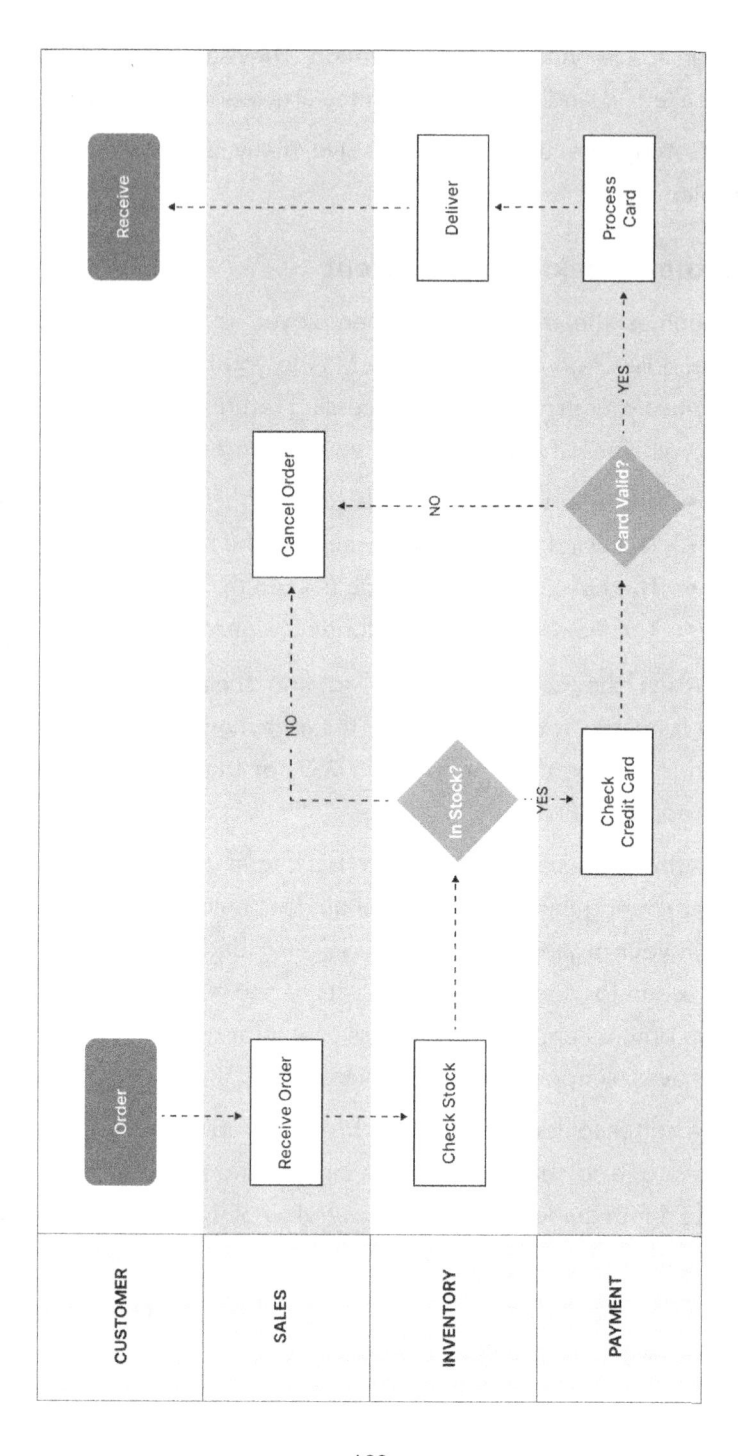

Each swim lane represents a different department or role in your organization. As you map out the process, you can diagram how the process flows between roles or departments. This is a wonderful *planning* tool, but it is not a *doing* tool. We will transfer knowledge faster if we focus on helping people *do* things. Each time a process crosses a swim lane, you should have a new article that is just for that specific role.

A good way of thinking about this is to consider what situations the specific role is responding to. For example, if we looked at the customer service agent role in the above process, we might have the following guides:

- How to prepare an RMA when a customer requests a refund
- How to respond to a customer who asks if their RMA has arrived yet
- What to do when the QA team approves or rejects a return
- How to respond when a customer asks for the status of their refund

Each article deals with a specific context. By breaking things up this way, it is much easier for the agent to find the guidance they need.

You should never have a situation where an employee needs to start in the middle of a guide. If you do, then you need to break those guides apart.

Step 2: Making It Followable

What Do You Include in the Guide?

This is the part where people get into trouble—deciding what should and shouldn't go in the guide. You have to perform a delicate balancing act. Put too much detail in, and people won't use the guide. But if you put too little detail in, they won't be able to work independently.

Here are the most common mistakes we see when deciding what to include or leave out of a digital guide:

- Including too much background information or foundational knowledge
- Presenting the same level of detail to everyone (both new and experienced employees)
- Not accounting for all the actual variables that an employee would have to deal with in a real situation

So, how do you avoid those mistakes?

1. Leave out the foundational knowledge
2. Design for repeated use
3. Deal with the variables

Leave Out the Foundational Knowledge

The biggest improvement you can make to your guides is to leave out anything that can be categorized as foundational knowledge.

Have you ever played laser tag? If you go to the laser tag arena and play 10 rounds in a row, you still need to sit through the introduction video every time. What a bummer. You are ready to get right back in and start zapping people, but instead, you have to sit through the same five-minute video you have already seen six times.

Your employees feel the same way when you include foundational information in your digital guides. Go back to the workshop report you created and look at all the information in the right "Process/Concepts" column. None of that should be included in the digital guide. That is information you expect the employee to know *before* they use your digital guides.

You may choose to include a link to a separate article that covers the foundational material, but don't include the foundational material in the guide itself.

For example, if you have a guide on how to create a new loan application, you don't need to include information about why you are creating the application, what the loan application software helps the business do, or the regulations around loan processing. Remember, we are just creating recipes. Just give them the ingredients and the steps they need to bake the cake. Don't tell them all about how your great-grandmother used to make it every Sunday.

Common things you will want to keep out of your guides:

- Anecdotes
- Explanations of concepts
- Historical information
- Commentary

Your employees need to find, follow, and scan these pretty quickly, so we don't want to have any extra bloat in there.

Design for Repeated Use

You want your employees to use your digital guides every time they perform any task that is even slightly complex.

Why? Because the digital guides:

- Eliminate mistakes
- Help employees work faster
- Help employees work with more confidence
- Allow employees to instantly adapt to changes

But if your digital guides are too long and cumbersome to use, your employees will start working from memory.

> **TIPS FROM THE TRENCHES**
>
> Do they really need to follow digital guides every time they complete a task?
>
> The answer is … it depends.
>
> We like to consider three aspects of a task to determine if an employee needs to regularly use a guide: Complexity, Length, and Frequency.
>
> Employees should always use a guide for tasks of even moderate complexity. They will work faster and will produce fewer mistakes.
>
> If a task is long (i.e., it contains many steps), then an employee should always use a digital guide.
>
> If a task is only performed infrequently, for example, once a week, once or month, or once a year, the employee should always use a digital guide.
>
> But if a task is short, has a low level of complexity, and is performed on almost a daily basis, then repeated use of digital guides doesn't need to be required.
>
> Ultimately, you want to let performance dictate what you require. Are your employees completing tasks efficiently and correctly without using digital guides? Then don't require the use of digital guides for those tasks.
>
> But if mistakes are being made or tasks are taking too long, hold your employees accountable for using the digital guides.

The solution is to design the guides so that experienced employees can quickly navigate them. At the same time, you want to allow new or less experienced employees to easily access additional details. We want to design guides that work for both repeat and first-time users.

The following chart will help you determine which type of guide to create based on the type of activity you need to enable.

Type of Activity	Digital Guide Design
Lengthy procedure with no if/then situations	Use a checklist or bulleted list for each step. Allow a user to drill into each step to expose additional details.
Simple or lengthy task with multiple if/then stations or branches	Use a decision tree, but limit the amount of detail. Allow a user to drill into individual steps to expose more details if necessary.
Answer a simple question	Use a standard article.
Answer a complex question (multiple if/then variables)	Use a decision tree.
Troubleshooting guide	Use a decision tree.
Look up reference information	Use a standard article.

Cover the Variables

Your digital guides need to cover all the variables an employee might encounter. Variables can be exceptions, problems, or policies that apply to different situations. For example, if someone were calling in to reschedule a medical appointment, here are just a few variables that might apply:

1. Are you speaking to the person who is scheduled for the appointment or someone else? If it is someone else, do you have permission to speak with them?
2. How many days before the appointment are they contacting you? Do you have a policy for rescheduling within x number of days of the appointment?

You may need to address other edge cases as well, such as:

- What does the employee do if they can't find the appointment in the system?
- What do they do if the patient asks for the late change fee to be waived?

- What do they do if this is an urgent issue, but they can't find another appointment time within the next week?

All of this should have been identified during your workshop, but inevitably some variables get missed. As you are building the digital guide, anticipate these situations and work to cover them.

By handling all the variables in a given activity, you ensure that everyone on your team will be able to follow your procedures correctly.

The Importance of Decision Trees

Digital guides or help articles that involve multiple variables can be a training nightmare. Employees have to read the guides multiple times just to figure out which set of rules they should apply. Or employees have to go through dozens of repeated transactions over the course of several months so they can learn by experience what needs to be done.

Decision trees can completely eliminate employee errors while drastically reducing the time it takes to perform tasks. We had one customer that reduced the time it took to troubleshoot an issue from 20 minutes down to 6 minutes just by adding a decision tree.

Decision trees can be applied to a variety of situations:

- Call flows
- Procedures or tasks that are impacted by multiple variables
- The correct application of complex policies to a situation
- Troubleshooting problems

If you are ever tempted to write "If ... then ..." in any sort of training material, you should consider replacing it with a decision tree.

The Prepare System Part 2 – Design + Refine

Let's look at an example. Here is a procedure written without using a decision tree:

> If this is a residential account, you will need to make sure that you have proof of address for the customer. If this is a commercial address, then you need to have proof of address and a business license.
>
> For residential accounts:
>
> - Ask for proof of address.
> - Scan the document.
> - Attach it to the customer record.
>
> For commercial accounts:
>
> - Ask for proof of address.
> - Ask for business license.
> - Scan the documents.
> - Attach them to the customer record.
>
> Also, make sure that if it's a residential account that you are talking to, you have the document scanned to the "Internal" folder on the shared drive. If it's a commercial account, you don't need to upload the document—just send it to Steve, and he'll do it for you.

In this book, we can't totally recreate the experience of a digital decision tree, but this example should give you an idea of how it can be simplified:

> What type of account is this?
>
> - Residential
> - Commercial

> Scan this QR code to see an interactive example of this decision tree.
>
> www.screensteps.com/find-follow-book/resources/decision-tree-example

Once employees select the correct answer, they are presented with just the steps that pertain to that situation. Additional follow-up questions can be asked to further guide the employee.

Step 3: Making It Scannable

Once your guides are findable and followable, it is time to go back and make them scannable. We all know that people don't really read content on the web. They scan it. This is especially true when an employee is working in a high-stress situation or under pressure to complete something quickly.

Here are some tips for making your articles more scannable.

Write for Action

Most documentation is too verbose. Remember the end goal—we want employees to be able to *do* things. You will not be penalized for using incomplete sentences.

Use action verbs such as "Click here," "Ask this," "Go there," and "Decide that." Be as succinct as possible.

Bad:

When you receive a new purchase order, you need to create an invoice that contains the PO number on it.

Better:

When you receive a purchase order:

- Create an invoice
- Add the PO#

Include Headings

Break your content up with headings. Headings should allow the employee to quickly scan the guide and understand the major sections. Headings aren't just bolded text. You should use actual headings that create logical sections for your guide.

Use Bullets Instead of Commas

Don't ever put a series of tasks into a comma-separated list.

Bad:

Go to the invoices screen, filter for unpaid invoices, click on each invoice, and send a follow-up.

Better:

- Go to invoices screen.
- Filter for unpaid invoices.
- Click on each invoice.
- Send follow-up.

Add Screenshots

Screenshots make employees' brains do less work. That is a great thing! Use them.

When you write, "Click the 'Schedule an appointment button,'" your employee has to read the text, understand it, and then search for a button that has that text on their screen.

If you use a screenshot, then their brains don't have to do any of that conversion from text to visuals.

Sometimes we hear people say, "But what if the screens change?"

Let's look at that scenario. Imagine you have a process that tells an employee to click on the "Schedule follow-ups" button.

Imagine two guides, one with screenshots and one without.

Then imagine that the software you are using removes the button or renames it.

The person following the text-only guide is going to waste time trying to find the button on the page. Since they don't have a visual picture to refer to, they have to play hide and seek with a button that no longer exists.

The person following the guide with screenshots instantly knows that something has changed. They can comment on the guide and let the content owner know it needs to be updated. And if the interface is somewhat the same, the person following the guide may be able to discern where the button is even though it's not a perfect match.

Which scenario is going to result in better performance by your employees?

Use screenshots, and use them liberally.

Use Checklists

Checklists are a fantastic tool for longer processes. Don't include too much text in the checklist. Ideally, you would put any additional instructions as an expandable section under the checklist item. The checklist should be detailed enough that if someone follows it, they will complete the process correctly, but not so detailed that it bogs down the employee.

Bad:
- ✓ Click contacts.
- ✓ Click new contact.
- ✓ Enter first name.
- ✓ Enter last name.
- ✓ Enter phone number.
- ✓ Add billing information.
- ✓ Save.

Better:
- ✓ Create a new contact.
- ✓ Enter name and phone number.
- ✓ Add billing information.
- ✓ Save.

Try Styled Text

Styled text can be very effective in highlighting important points. You can use bold, italic, colored text, or text with a colored background. In our guides, we include blocks of text with colored backgrounds for warnings, alerts, tips, and additional information.

The most important thing is to not overuse styled text. There is a famous quote from Syndrome in the movie *The Incredibles*, "When everyone's super, no one will be." You may or may not agree with that sentiment when it comes to people, but it is definitely true when it comes to your text formatting.

I have seen client documentation where 90% of the words are highlighted in red. Why? They say they want to make sure that their employees don't miss anything. It's all important!

Well, if you make everything important, then eventually, your employees' eyes just start seeing everything as the same.

Use styled text judiciously. It should be used infrequently enough that when your employees do see styled text, they know they need to pay extra attention.

Use Collapsible Sections

Collapsible sections are headings of text that, when clicked on, expand to show additional text or images. Sometimes, they are called "accordions" because of the way they fold out.

Scan this QR code to see an example of what collapsible sections look like.

[QR code]

www.screensteps.com/find-follow-book/resources/collapsible-sections

---

Collapsible sections are great tools for presenting optional information. They can really help when you are trying to create a single guide that will work for both new users and experienced users. They are also good if you have some information that your company requires to be present in every guide, but that isn't really actionable.

It is not uncommon for us to see documentation that is filled with a page and a half or more of background information before we ever get to the actual instructions. There will be parts about who authored it, when it was updated, who the audience is, what regulations it relies on, etc. This is information that is primarily useful to the author or the manager reviewing the guide. It is not useful at all to the person who has to follow it. I just recently viewed a six-page piece of documentation for a process that had only three steps. It took six pages before I got to a bullet list of three items. That is certainly not scannable.

A great solution is to stick this content into a collapsible section at the top of the guide. That way, those who need it can quickly access it, but employees who are just trying to follow instructions aren't burdened with it.

Another way we like to use collapsible sections is for a "You should see this" section. Remember that we want to keep our guides very actionable. A newer user may want to verify that they are doing things correctly, so a collapsible section that has a screenshot of what they should see at a certain point in the process can be very helpful. By putting it in a collapsible section, we still keep the guide scannable for more experienced employees.

Include Links

Another great way to keep your guides scannable is to replace sub-sections that go into the edge cases with links to other guides that specifically address the edge case. Maybe you are making a guide on how to track a delivery for a customer. You use multiple carriers, so there are a lot of variables involved. But in rare cases, a customer calls in, and the employee can't find them in the system. Instead of including instructions on what to do in that situation in the main guide, create a separate guide titled "What to Do When You Can't Find a Customer in the System" and add a link from your main guide.

This keeps your primary guide from getting bogged down with all the details about the edge cases while still giving the employee easy access to those instructions in case they need them.

With some dedicated focus on making your guides scannable, you will increase the productivity of your employees (less time reading and more time doing) and, at the same time, decrease their mistakes.

> TIPS FROM THE TRENCHES
>
> It can be really helpful to develop a style guide for your knowledge base. For some tips on developing a style guide, read our article here:
>
> blog.screensteps.com/include-knowledge-base-style-guide

Acceptance Testing

A new digital guide isn't ready until it has been tested by someone who didn't write the guide. We call this acceptance testing.

To perform acceptance testing, find someone who did not author the guide and do the following:

1. Have them follow the guide.
2. Don't give any additional commentary. Any additional guidance you give is the equivalent of tribal knowledge and represents a failure in the guide.
3. Are there areas where the employee gets stuck or confused? Update the guide and test it again.

> TIPS FROM THE TRENCHES
>
> If your employees are not used to following digital guides, you will need to give a brief explanation of what the guides do and how they work. After five minutes of getting used to decision trees, collapsible sections, tips, links, etc., they have enough foundational knowledge to begin using your guides and testing them out.

Depending on the knowledge base software you are using, you should be able to update and retest this guide in real time. By testing and iterating, you will fine-tune a guide very quickly and ensure that it will help employees perform activities successfully.

When a digital guide can be followed successfully by an employee with no additional assistance, then it is ready to be released into production.

Summary

- It isn't enough to just write down information. You need to design digital guides that are findable, followable, and scannable.
- Separate foundational and actionable knowledge in your guides.
- Break up your digital guides and improve their titles to make them more findable.
- Make your guides more followable by covering all the variables and designing them for repeated use.
- Make your guides more scannable by using the formatting tips in this chapter.
- Make sure that you test your guides with real users.

Now that you understand how to use the Prepare System to

build out your digital guides, it's time to talk about incorporating these guides into your training processes. That is done using the Train System, which we will cover next.

Chapter 12:

The Train System

In this chapter, you will learn:

- The concepts behind the Train System and how they will help you train new and existing employees more efficiently
- How to separate your training into topic areas
- How to prepare foundational courses and practice activities
- How to run Find & Follow Training sessions

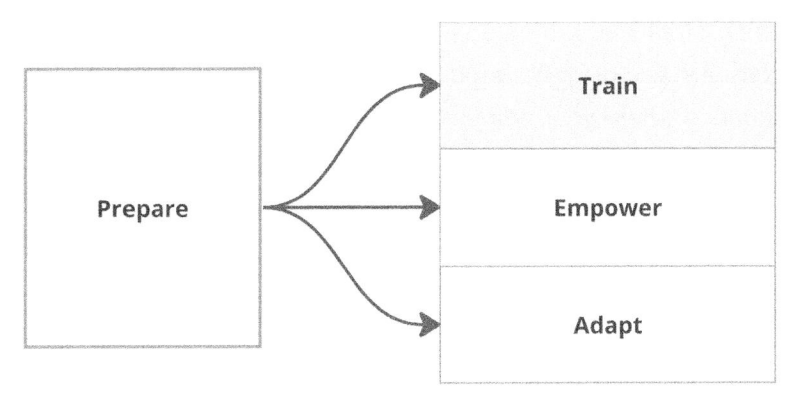

The Train System

Unless your organization is completely static, you know the pain that is involved in training new employees. New hires not only take a long time to become fully productive, but while they are getting up to speed, they bring down the productivity of everyone around them.

Why? Because they always need help with something. Or, if they don't ask for help, they do something wrong that needs to be fixed by someone with more experience.

The Train System in Find & Follow will solve that problem. It will address your most frustrating training needs. New hires will onboard faster. Transformational changes will be implemented with much less pain and almost no loss in productivity.

The Train System consists of four parts:

1. Break Up the Topics
2. Prepare Foundational Courses
3. Prepare Practice Activities
4. Run Find & Follow Training Sessions

We will explain each of these tasks in this chapter.

Break Up the Topics

Think of all the information that your new employees have to consume as a giant buffet. But unlike a normal buffet, this isn't a situation where your employees can just pick and choose which items they want to eat. They have to eventually eat all of it.

Trying to gobble it all up in one sitting is going to lead to some very unhappy employees and a messy buffet floor.

As they say, the best way to eat an elephant is one bite at a time.

We can make the buffet much more manageable if we break up our training materials into topic areas. For example, if I were training a group of credit union employees, I might break up the topics as follows:

1. What Credit Unions Do
2. Savings & CDs
3. Personal Loans
4. Personal Cards
5. Safe Deposit Boxes
6. Etc.

As we run the training, we will complete the following sequence of activities for each topic area:

- Lay the Foundation
- Introduce the Tools
- Practice the Activities

For each topic area, you will spend:

- 10–20% of your time teaching foundational material
- A few minutes becoming familiar with the digital guides for that topic area
- 80–90% of your time practicing real-world scenarios (activities) while using the digital guides

Prepare Foundational Courses

Foundational courses will give your employees the background knowledge they need to successfully follow the digital guides. Foundational courses are much different than traditional courses. They are shorter, require very little memorization, and don't cover any step-by-step procedures.

Most traditional courses we see consist of hour-long video recordings, PowerPoint decks with 100+ slides, or classroom lecture plans that go on for days. The table below outlines some of the differences between typical courses we see in the workplace and foundational courses.

	Typical Course	Foundational Course
Duration	1 hour or more	10–30 minutes (ideally 20)
# of slides	100+	Around 20
Level of detail	Click-by-click instructions, lots of screenshots, lots of text	High-level concepts, analogies, and stories

When Do You Need Foundational Courses?

You will use foundational courses in three situations:

1. When you are going through a Transformational Change (e.g., new CRM/ERP system)
2. When you are training new employees
3. When you are training employees on something new (e.g., cross-training)

What Do You Include in Your Foundational Course?

To know what to include in your foundational course, just go back to your planning worksheet. The right column that lists the processes and concepts will contain all the information you need to cover in your foundational courses. Everything in the other columns should *not* be included in your course. The other columns belong in your digital guides.

Foundational Courses for Transformational Change

When you are building a training for a transformational change, your foundational courses will cover key concepts of the new software or process. You don't want to get into the low-level details at all. The digital guides will take care of that.

If I were preparing training for a new CRM rollout, I might have foundational courses around the following topics:

- Why are we making this change?
- What are the different parts of the new CRM?
- What will change for an employee's specific role?

Foundational Courses for New Hire Training

If I were preparing foundational courses for a new hire training program, I would cover the following topics:

- What does our company do?
- Who are our customers?
- What tools will you be using on your job?
- What concepts do you need to understand about our industry?

Options for Delivering Foundational Courses

Delivering foundational courses does not need to be complicated. We have found these three methods to be effective:

- Instructor-led slide presentations
- Videos
- Text-based courses

Instructor-led Slide Presentations

If you are only going to be training new hires infrequently, then an instructor-led slide presentation is by far the easiest solution. We have all suffered death by PowerPoint, but if you follow the principles explained above, your foundational courses will be short and focused. Your employees will jump into practice activities so quickly that they won't have time to be bored. Each foundational course should have a maximum of 20–30 slides.

Videos

If you are going to be running repeated trainings, then it is worth recording your foundational courses. Just use the same slide deck and talk through the presentation. If you're using online software to present the course, break up the videos into separate segments. When we prepare foundational courses, we typically have course segments that are about 2–3 minutes long.

Text-based Courses
The last option is to create text-based course material. We really look at this as a last resort. It isn't nearly as engaging as instructor-led or video courses, but it will still work if that is your only option.

Prepare Practice Activities

Gaining Confidence in Using the Digital Guides
Now that you have prepared your digital guides and foundational courses, it is time to start working on your practice activities.

Practice activities help employees gain confidence when using the digital guides. These practice activities should mirror real-world situations that employees will encounter.

As employees gain experience using the digital guides, they will gain confidence in their ability to work independently.

We had a customer come to us once and tell us that before applying Find & Follow principles, new hires in their contact center would often break down in tears during training because they were so scared to take their first call. These new agents had no confidence in their ability to handle a call on their own.

Compare that to another contact center that used the Find & Follow Framework to train their new agents. They had agents *asking* to take calls a week before they were supposed to get out of training.

Employees that successfully complete practice activities are eager to get to work, while those who don't are terrified to be left on their own.

What Is the Measure of Success?
The measure of success for practice sessions is whether or not the employee can successfully follow the digital guides to complete

multiple practice activities without making mistakes and without needing assistance.

It is not required that they complete a practice activity for every possible scenario or even every guide that you have created. The goal is for them to be comfortable and confident following your digital guides.

How to Determine Your Practice Activities

The list of practice activities should be taken from the "Activities" column of your Find & Follow Report. For each activity in the list, we would create different scenarios that would account for each variation of that job, question, request, or problem.

For example, if we were working in medical billing, we might have activities that include the following tasks:

- Look up a patient record.
- Verify insurance.
- Apply a payment to a patient bill.

To help build the practice activities, we would want to account for many of the variations the employee might encounter.

Here are some examples.

Task	Scenarios
Look up a patient record.	• A patient calls up to check the amount they owe. • The spouse of a patient calls up to check the amount they owe. • The child or parent of a patient calls up to check the amount they owe. • No patient record exists for the person calling.
Verify insurance.	• Each insurance carrier may have a different process for verifying insurance. Create scenarios for multiple insurance carriers. • The insurance is verifiable. • The patient has insurance with the carrier but has a co-pay. • The patient has verifiable insurance, and there is no co-pay. • The patient's record does not exist in the insurer's system.
Apply a payment to a patient bill.	• The payment is for the full amount. • The payment is for less than the bill amount. • The payment is for more than the bill amount. • A payment is made, but you can't find the invoice to apply it to.

As you can see, for each of these tasks, there are multiple scenarios that could throw a new employee for a loop. The more variables we can cover during training, the more comfortable employees will be when those variables show up later in their actual day-to-day job.

Run the Find & Follow Training Sessions

You will go through the following progression for each topic area as you work through the practice activities:

1. Practice finding the right guides
2. Practice following them

But the first few topics you go through, you may need to break this down even more.

When it comes to practicing following the guides, we've found it helpful to first have employees become comfortable with the design of the guides by reading through a few of them on their own. This is a little like wading into a pool instead of just diving right in.

So for the first few topics, you will go through the following four stages in your practice activities:

1. Finding
2. Reviewing
3. Following
4. Practicing

Finding

If your employees can't find the right guide, then the whole Find & Follow Framework breaks down pretty quickly. Start by just asking employees to find guides based on scenarios you present to them.

At first, don't have them use the search. Just have them browse for the guide in your table of contents. This will help them get a sense of how the knowledge base is organized.

After they have had a bit of practice finding guides in the table of contents, then move on to asking them to search for guides.

You don't need to spend long here but don't skip this step.

Reviewing

Now that they can find the right guides, have them read through several and talk you through what they would do. Don't have them actually do anything yet. They are just going to explain what they would do if they were following the guide.

At this stage, they are getting used to how the guide is formatted without feeling any pressure to do anything correctly.

You may find that they skip steps or miss instructions. That's all right. Let them make the mistakes, and then ask them to go back and see if they missed anything.

Don't tell them what to do. They need to be able to follow the guide, so let them go through it a few times until they can talk you through it without skipping key steps.

Following

Next, have them actually follow a guide to do something. This could be a software task in a sandbox environment or some other scenario you present. They are learning to go from just reading the guide to actually following it.

Practicing

After employees are proficient at using the guides to complete tasks, then have them go through realistic scenarios that they will experience on the job. If they interact with customers, pretend to be a customer calling them up or walking up to them and asking a question. The learner will have to pull up the correct guide and follow it with the added stress of having you waiting on them.

TIPS FROM THE TRENCHES

We have found that for the first few topics, you need to spend some time in the Finding and Reviewing stages. But after a few times of practicing, you won't have to spend much time on those activities for the other topics. For the other topics, you will just spend your time finding and following the guides.

By the end of these progressions, employees will be very well prepared to join the workforce and begin taking on actual jobs.

Example Training Agenda

Here is an example of what a Find & Follow Training agenda might look like.

Training Curriculum for New Hires at Bank

Day 1	• Welcome (60 minutes) • Ice breakers (60 minutes) • Core Systems Check (60 minutes) • Lunch (60 minutes) • HR Onboarding (120 minutes) • Introduction to training (60 minutes) • Meet your team (60 minutes) • **Introduction to ScreenSteps** (60 minutes)
Day 2	• Welcome/explanation of training (30 minutes) • **Course**: Banking Overview (20 minutes) • **Activities**: Banking Overview Discussion (60 minutes) • **Course**: Banking System (15 minutes) • **Activities**: Navigating around (60 minutes) • **Course**: Checking (15 minutes) • **Activities**: Checking Scenarios (2 hours) • Lunch • **Course**: Savings & CDs (15 minutes) • **Activities**: Savings & CDs (2 hours)

Day 3	• Welcome/follow-up questions (20 minutes)
	• **Course**: Personal Loans (20 minutes)
	• **Activities**: Personal Loans Activities (3 hours)
	• Lunch
	• **Course**: Personal Cards (15 minutes)
	• **Activities**: Personal Cards (2 hours)
Day 4	• Welcome/follow-up questions
	• **Course:** Online & Mobile Banking (20 minutes)
	• **Activities**: Online & Mobile Banking (2 hours)
	• Lunch
	• **Course**: Safe Deposit Boxes (15 minutes)
	• **Activities**: Safe Deposit Boxes activities (60 minutes)
Day 5	• Daily Tasks (60 minutes)
	• **Course**: Soft Skills (15 minutes)
	• **Activities**: Soft Skills Practice (2 hours)
	• Lunch
	• **Activities**: Rapid-fire simple questions (60 minutes)
	• **Activities**: Complex questions (90 minutes)
	• **Celebrate**: Until it's time to go home

Summary

- Break up your topics during training to make your training more digestible.
- Create foundational courses that are 10-30 minutes in length and that only teach foundational knowledge (not actionable knowledge)
- Prepare practice activities that mirror real-world scenarios
- During training sessions do the following with your trainers:
  - Present the foundational material
  - Introduce the digital guides
  - Allow them to practice using the digital guides to handle the practice activities you prepared

Now that you know how to use the Train System to train your employees you're all set, right? Wrong! Training isn't enough! To really get the benefits of Find & Follow you have to change the way your employees work. The Empower System will give you the tools you need to ensure that employees and supervisors adopt this new way of working and that is what we will cover next.

Chapter 13:

The Empower System

In this chapter, you will learn:

- The concepts behind the Empower System
- How to encourage employees to rely on the digital guides
- How to stop answering the same questions all day long and increase employee independence
- How to invest your time in creating reusable digital guides

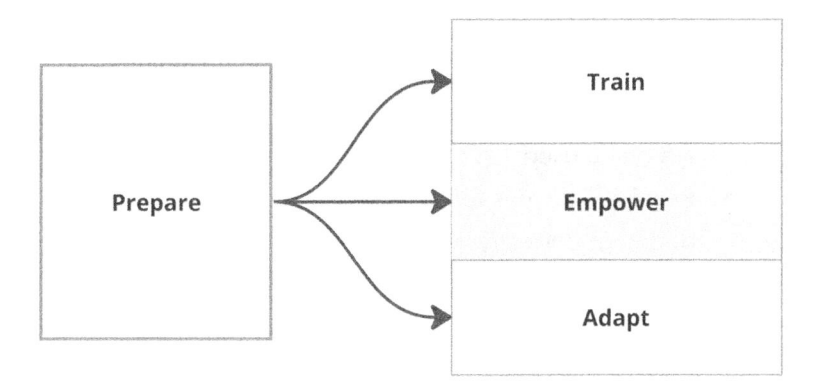

Prepare	Train
	Empower
	Adapt

We all know that just because employees are taught a certain way of working doesn't mean they will stick with it. We have seen that right when organizations are starting to see success with Find & Follow, they sometimes let their guard down and start falling back into tribal knowledge habits.

The components in the Empower System will ensure that your Find & Follow program keeps firing on all cylinders.

The Empower System has three components:

- Rely on the Digital Guides
- Redirect Questions
- Invest In Reusable Knowledge

These components really build on the topics we covered in Prepare and Train, but it is crucial that they are reinforced on an ongoing basis if the new behaviors are going to stick.

Rely on Digital Guides

Employees need to continue relying on digital guides as they perform their work. Unless supervisors set clear expectations, employees will believe that you want them to eventually stop using the guides.

Once your employees start relying on their memories again, you will immediately notice your metrics start to dip.

How do you help employees rely on the digital guides?

- Regularly review reports to ensure your digital guides are being used.
- Praise employees for demonstrating the commitment to do things correctly.
- DON'T praise employees for working from memory.
- Hold employees accountable for making mistakes when they consistently choose not to use the digital guides.

If supervisors set the expectation that employees use the digital guides on a regular basis, then employees will use them. If the use of the guides is seen as purely optional, then employees will revert to tribal knowledge.

Redirect Questions

One of the key moments when supervisors can strengthen or sabotage your Find & Follow culture is when an employee asks them a question. If they respond to the email, answer the chat message, or tell the employee what to do, then the employee will learn to rely on tribal knowledge.

The key is to redirect, but this can be tricky. Supervisors want to be helpful, and it can sometimes seem harsh or uncaring to redirect an employee to your knowledge base.

The key is in how you do it. Here are some tips:

- Tell the employee that you want to make sure they can succeed if you are out of the office or unavailable. Then ask them if they have tried to find a digital guide with the answer in the knowledge base.
- If time is of the essence, find the digital guide for them and send them a link to the guide.
- If the employee has found the digital guide but is struggling to understand it, take a moment to see where the problem is. If necessary, update the guide to clarify it further and ask the employee if the changes make things easier.
- If the employee is struggling to find the information they need, either make an article request or make a note to work on improving the findability of the article the employee needs.

If the supervisor responds with a genuine desire to help the employee gain independence and not simply with a "Why are you bothering me?" attitude, their team will eventually start turning to the digital guides first and will only come to the supervisor when a digital guide doesn't exist for the situation they are in.

Invest in Reusable Knowledge

The way supervisors work will shift under Find & Follow. Whenever a supervisor answers a question, it is like paying rent instead of building equity. Creating or updating digital guides is akin to building equity that will provide wealth in the future.

You want supervisors who build equity instead of pay rent.

There will be situations where a digital guide doesn't exist. So, what do you do when a situation comes up that isn't covered in a digital guide?

Follow these rules:

- If the employee needs an answer right away and the supervisor has time, create a new digital guide right in that moment. If you have the right tools, this will be faster than writing an email or writing out a chat response.
- If the employee needs an answer right away but the supervisor is not able to create a digital guide in that moment, guide the employee but capture a note to create the digital guide later.
- If the employee can wait, then make a note to create the digital guide later and send it to the employee.

It can be helpful to have some sort of tracking system to track digital guides that need to be created.

Summary

- You will empower your employees as you reinforce the importance of relying on digital guides, even after training.
- Supervisors need to build "knowledge equity" by updating existing guides and creating new ones instead of just answering questions.

Now that supervisors are helping your team be knowledgeable, efficient, and independent, there is one more thing that can bring the whole system to its knees—*change*. But don't worry! We will learn how to tame that demon in the next chapter.

Chapter 14:

The Adapt System

In this chapter, you will learn:

- How to use the Adapt System to respond to change
- How to decrease the time your employees have to spend in training when a change occurs

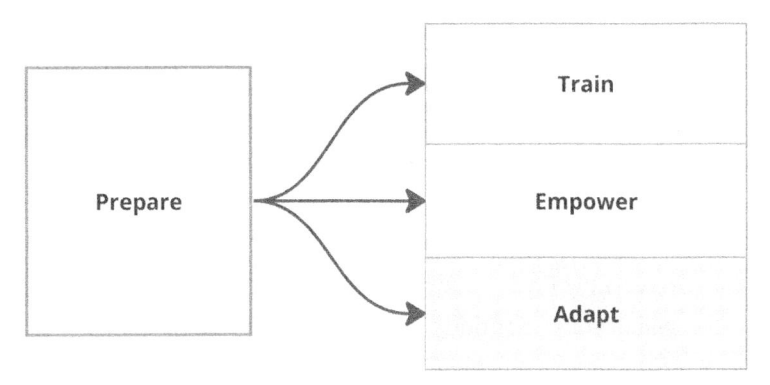

Prepare	Train
	Empower
	Adapt

So far, we have lived in a mostly perfect world where we had to deal with very little change. Maybe a guide was missing or incomplete, but the Empower System gives us the tools to handle those situations.

But what happens when things change? It could be new regulations, a major software update, a merger, or some other transformational change. How can we adapt in Find & Follow?

Don't worry. You already have all the tools you will need to adapt to ongoing and transformational change in the Adapt System.

The Adapt System has three components:
- Analyze the Impact
- Prepare the Guides
- Notify or Train

Analyze the Impact

When you recognize that a change is coming to your organization, the first step is to analyze the impact.

Some changes, like a new CRM or ERP, may impact almost every task for certain roles in your organization. Others, like a temporary office closing, may just impact a few of your digital guides.

Here are some tips for analyzing the impact:

- Review the list of activities, sub-tasks, and variables in your Find & Follow Workshop Report. Reviewing this list will help you identify which guides need to be updated.
- If the change is significant, it may be worth running a new Find & Follow Workshop. This will ensure that you have fully understood what new information employees will need to continue working independently.
- If the change is minor, simply identify the guides that will need to be updated.

Prepare the Guides

At this point, most organizations would start preparing materials for a lunch and learn or a company town hall.

But as a Find & Follow Organization, you don't need to drag your employees through a mind-numbing PowerPoint presentation. Find & Follow has prepared your organization for just this moment.

Instead of just *telling* people about all the changes, just update the guides. Make sure that any changes are clear. If the changes are particularly minor, you may want to call them out in some way.

But be careful. We have seen organizations that really go overboard here. When every line is red because the Knowledge Champion is trying to highlight the changes, the red font color really loses its effectiveness.

If everything in the guide has changed, just put a note at the top that the majority of the guide has changed, signaling to employees that they should pay special attention as they use the guide.

Notify or Train

Once you have updated the guides, you need to decide if you need to use the Train System to retrain employees or if you just need to notify them of the change.

Here are some suggestions for making that decision:
- If the change will not require new foundational knowledge, just make an adjustment to the actionable knowledge in the digital guides. Then send employees a notification that the guide has changed. If employees are using the guides regularly, then they will be able to adapt very easily to the new procedures.
- If the change will require new foundational knowledge, then use the Train System to build out the foundational courses and retrain your employees.

The main point is to only provide new training if you absolutely need to. In most cases, you will find that updating the guides and notifying your employees of the change is sufficient.

> **Summary**
> - When change happens, first analyze the impact of the change to determine which guides will need to be updated.
> - Update the digital guides as needed, highlighting important changes if necessary.
> - Don't overdo it when highlighting changes.
> - If employees will need additional foundational knowledge, use the Train System to retrain them.
> - If additional foundational knowledge is not required, then just notify employees that certain procedures have changed.

That's it! We have covered all four of the Find & Follow systems. Next, we are going to discuss how to launch your Find & Follow program.

Part V:

Applying Find & Follow to Real Problems

Knowledge is power, but knowledge sharing is empowerment." – Anonymous

In this section, we are going to look at some real-world situations and show you how you could use the Find & Follow Framework to make significant improvements. As stated at the beginning of the book, many of these examples will come from contact centers due to the abundance of data that can be found there.

Chapter 15:

Decreasing the Load on Tier 2 Reps

In this chapter, you will learn how Find & Follow helps decrease the load on Tier 2 reps, including:

- Resolving issues in less time
- Decreasing escalations
- Decreasing Tier 2 training time

Tier 2 reps are often overburdened. Anything that Tier 1 can't handle gets escalated to them. They often have queues that are backed up with customer issues that need to get resolved.

Applying Find & Follow can help Tier 2 reps in the following ways:

1. It can help them resolve issues in less time.
2. It can decrease escalations from Tier 1 to Tier 2.
3. It can decrease the time it takes to train up additional Tier 2 reps.

Let's look at each situation.

Resolving Issues in Less Time

When you create digital guides for the most common situations that Tier 2 reps need to deal with, you will see an instant improvement in the consistency of how each rep approaches the same situation. Once you have consistency, you can begin to iterate on the procedure incorporating feedback and ideas from the Tier 2 team themselves.

As you continue to iterate and improve the guide, you will see the average time to solve the issue decrease across all reps. As I mentioned before, we had one customer who used this process and decreased average handle time by 70%. Another customer was able to continually improve their troubleshooting process because everything was documented in a digital guide. Allowing Tier 2 reps to resolve issues in less time greatly reduces stress across the entire contact center.

Decreasing Escalations

Issues get escalated to Tier 2 because Tier 2 reps have more knowledge and experience. They are also more expensive. It is better for everyone involved if the business is able to decrease escalations to the Tier 2 team. It means less stress for the Tier 2 team, fewer customers waiting for a resolution, more productivity out of the Tier 1 team, and a lower average cost per resolution for the business.

By analyzing the way Tier 2 reps approach a complicated situation and capturing it in a decision tree, you can allow Tier 1 agents to solve problems that previously only Tier 2 reps could handle. We call these Expert Guides because they allow non-experts to solve problems as if they had expert knowledge.

Tier 1 teams won't need extensive training. They just need to be taught to find and follow the digital guides that will help them resolve the issue. Even if the case eventually gets escalated, the Tier 1 rep will have already performed a lot of the troubleshooting, allowing the Tier 2 agent to skip over those tasks and start exploring other possible solutions.

This has a dramatic impact on the contact center. In one contact center, the Tier 1 agents jokingly asked their supervisors what the Tier 2 team was going to do now that they weren't escalating any calls to them. Another contact center found that new agents were just as able to handle complex situations as more tenured agents. Since all they needed to know how to do was follow the digital decision tree, it didn't really matter to them whether it was a complex or simple scenario. It is very similar to navigating with a GPS. It doesn't matter how many turns are involved. All you have to do is follow the directions.

Decreasing Tier 2 Training Time

Training a new Tier 2 rep can take a very long time and involves a lot of shadowing. This shadowing process decreases the productivity of the Tier 2 team, which is already stretched pretty thin.

By building a Find & Follow training program for the Tier 2 team, you can get new hires up to speed without burdening the existing team.

Because there are digital guides for Tier 2 reps to follow, those new reps can become productive as soon as they leave training, actually decreasing the load on other Tier 2 reps instead of increasing it.

Steps to Decrease Tier 2 Escalations

- Run a Find & Follow Workshop with members of your Tier 2 team.
- Identify which issues cause the most escalations.

- Work with the Tier 2 team to design digital guides that will allow the Tier 1 team to resolve the issue without escalating.
- Let Tier 1 reps practice using the guides on some example scenarios.
- Launch the guides, gather feedback, and iterate until you eliminate the escalations.

Summary

Organizations that adopt Find & Follow will see the following benefits for their Tier 2 teams:

- Less time spent on lower-value tasks/troubleshooting and more time spent on higher-value issues
- Lower time to resolution
- Less stress
- Greater consistency in how issues are handled

Tier 2 reps can also be a wonderful source of knowledge in designing your Find & Follow digital guides, allowing Tier 1 employees to resolve issues that could previously only be handled by the Tier 2 team.

Chapter 16:

Scaling Your Contact Center

In this chapter, you will learn how Find & Follow can help you scale your contact center while accomplishing the following:

- Scaling headcount more efficiently
- Creating a repeatable training program that reduces training costs
- Ensuring consistency in employee performance as you scale
- Reducing new-hire attrition

Scaling up a contact center that is operating at either the Tribal or Document Stage is extremely difficult. When a team is small, it is easy to operate on a Tribal Stage. New agents can observe more experienced agents or ask co-workers and supervisors for assistance. But as the team begins to scale, this Tribal approach and the knowledge bottleneck it creates quickly increases the weight and stress on supervisors and tenured agents.

For example, too many calls are coming in. To alleviate the problem, the organization hires more reps, but since each new rep needs to rely on a supervisor or tenured agent for guidance, each incremental new hire increases the workload on their more experienced counterparts.

Jim Gaffigan once quipped, "You know what it's like having four kids? Imagine you're drowning. And someone hands you a baby."

That is exactly how the supervisor feels in your growing contact center. They are already drowning, and you just handed them a group of new agents that don't know how to do anything. They will quickly sink.

This exact scenario often leads to burnout for supervisors or tenured employees and frustration and attrition among new hires. Service levels and quality scores plummet, and everything about the contact center feels very, very hard.

Find & Follow can help a scaling contact center in the following ways:

- Allowing the contact center to scale headcount more slowly
- Creating a repeatable training program that onboards new agents quickly and with a very low drag on supervisors or tenured agents
- Ensuring consistency in service offered as the contact center scales
- Reducing new hire attrition
- Faster and more effective cross-training

Scaling Headcount More Slowly

Most contact centers work to hit a target service level. A typical service level might be 80/30, meaning that 80% of the incoming calls are answered in 30 seconds or less. As call volumes increase, wait times increase, and service levels start to drop. For most contact centers that are faced with an increasing number of calls, the only option available to them is to hire more agents.

To know how many agents a contact center is going to need, supervisors and directors look at the total number of expected calls and the average time it takes to handle each of those calls. They then work backward to figure out what their headcount needs to be.

But there is another option. Any contact center that operates at the Tribal or Document Stage will see a decrease in the average time it takes to handle a call when they move to the Guide Stage of the Knowledge Ops Maturity Model. We have seen improvements as high as 70%.

By decreasing the time it takes to handle a call, you are essentially "hiring" more agents at no additional cost. For example, we had one client that was performing patient scheduling for a large group of medical offices that spanned several U.S. states. Prior to adopting Find & Follow, a typical agent could handle about 30 calls per shift.

After adopting Find & Follow, that number increased to between 70 and 80 calls per shift. This contact center more than doubled its workforce without hiring one additional employee!

They were in a rapid growth phase as well, so this increased productivity impacted all their hiring plans.

The ability to scale headcount more slowly has several impacts on the contact center:
- Lower headcount cost
- Lower recruiting and training costs
- Less stress on everyone as the contact center scales

Creating a Repeatable Training Program

Contact centers that are scaling rapidly are constantly training new agents. They have to train new hires to hit the projected staffing plan as well as train new hires to backfill agents who have left the organization. In many contact centers, new agent training can take three to eight weeks or even more. Achieving consistency between training classes can be difficult, especially if the contact center has multiple trainers.

But when you use the Find & Follow Framework to build a repeatable training program, everything becomes simpler.

The training program will consist of pre-determined foundational courses, digital guides, and practice activities. Trainers are not responsible for creating long lectures or presentations. In fact, trainers will spend very little time explaining concepts or procedures. The concepts will be taught in the foundational courses, and the procedures will be followed by using the digital guides. Trainers become facilitators instead of lecturers.

You will also see training times drop dramatically. We had one group that was scaling up a contact center. By adopting Find & Follow, they were able to cut training from six weeks to two weeks. And they did this all with a trainer who had no previous product knowledge. The trainer was able to come in, run the Find & Follow sessions using the foundational courses and practice activities, and successfully graduate knowledgeable, consistent, and efficient agents in just two weeks without having to be an expert on the products the contact center was supporting.

When you have a repeatable training program in place, new hires are no longer a burden on the organization. They rapidly get acclimated and instructed and become contributing employees.

Putting a repeatable training program in place will create the following outcomes:

- New agents will spend less time in training.
- Trainers will be able to train effectively with less domain expertise.
- Trainers and new hires will experience less stress.

- New agents will leave training better prepared to contribute to the contact center.

Ensuring Consistency in Service Offered

Have you ever played support agent roulette?

It's a game you play when you are speaking to an agent that clearly has no idea what they are talking about. You just hang up, call again, and hope you get someone else.

My oldest son is autistic and uses the Music application on his Mac in a very unique way. Unbeknownst to us, he added over 100,000 tracks to his library and brought the system to its knees. We got passed to one agent who started to tell me that I had to physically connect my son's Mac to my Mac up in my office to "re-sync" them. What? He did this all with a tone of voice that inspired no confidence at all. We asked to speak with another agent because he clearly had no idea what he was talking about.

We have another vendor that we purchase software from. They have grown very rapidly over the last few years. That growth has created a need for lots of new hires. Unfortunately, that means that the quality of the service we get from them has dropped dramatically.

The ironic thing is that they are a customer service company.

We no longer have any expectation of getting consistent answers from their support team. Someone is always checking with their supervisor or coming back to tell us that what they told us last week was incorrect. The entire support experience feels disorganized and chaotic.

The result? We are currently looking at other vendors and considering changing our support platform.

This is a clear sign that an organization was operating at the Tribal or Document Stage before it began to scale and is now struggling to catch up.

When you start operating at the Guide or Train Stage of the Knowledge Ops Maturity Model, service stays wonderfully consistent as you scale. Since each agent follows the same digital guides to answer questions, resolve problems, and apply policies, you, as a customer, can expect the same accurate, efficient, and consistent service, no matter how large the organization gets.

This consistency produces the following benefits:

- Higher NPS and CSAT scores
- Lower # of escalations
- Faster resolution times
- Less stress and greater confidence among agents

Reducing New Hire Attrition

New hire attrition costs contact centers a fortune. By the time a new agent starts training, the business has already spent money recruiting them. Unless they make it out of training and start successfully taking calls, all of that recruiting and training expense is wasted.

The worst scenario is when a new agent goes through all of training—especially six to eight weeks of training—and then quits. The contact center has to go back to the beginning, sourcing new candidates, hiring, and then training again. We have seen some cases where new-hire attrition can be as high as 87%.

Adopting Find & Follow has several impacts on new hire attrition. First, new hires spend less time in training. Every contact center is going to deal with new hire attrition, but it is much better that a new hire quit after two weeks of training instead of eight weeks of training.

Second, new hires spend very little time listening to lectures. They start practice activities right away. Trainers and the new hires themselves can assess very quickly whether or not the new agent will be able to follow the digital guides and successfully handle calls. Those agents that aren't going to work out are identified much sooner in the training process.

Third, and most importantly, Find & Follow makes working in the contact center much simpler and less stressful. This improved quality of the work environment leads to fewer agents quitting.

We had one client who told us that if their new agents didn't cry at some point during training, they knew that the agent wasn't understanding the true complexity of their job. The procedures were so complex and the situations so stressful that people were actually in tears as they prepared to take their first calls! How awful is that?

After adopting Find & Follow, everything became simpler. There were no more tears during training, and new hire attrition dropped from 87% to 17%.

Another BPO we worked with was in danger of losing their contract because they couldn't keep enough agents on the account. All the agents were quitting because the work was just too hard. They adopted Find & Follow, and soon the same account became the one all agents wanted to work on because it was so easy to know what to do. The staffing problems disappeared, and the account relationship was saved.

Reducing new hire attrition with the Find & Follow Framework saves thousands and sometimes millions of dollars in wasted recruiting, hiring, and training costs.

Faster and More Effective Cross-training

Many companies choose to specialize their contact center agents in specific departments. This is because they need to become familiar with a large amount of information to perform their jobs effectively. Additionally, certain departments may have higher call volumes than others. As a result, most contact centers aim to cross-train their agents, enabling them to assist other departments or regions during peak call periods.

However, cross-training is not without its challenges. When agents are selected for cross-training, they need to be taken off the line for a few weeks to learn how to handle calls for a different area within the company. This leads to a temporary decrease in available personnel.

Supervisors are faced with a decision: either hire more agents for each region or accept a temporary decrease in productivity as they try to cross-train additional agents.

This is a common scenario in Tribal or Document Stage organizations. However, things are entirely different when using the Find & Follow Framework.

With Find & Follow, agents are not required to memorize as much information, greatly simplifying the cross-training process. We worked with one contact center that dropped their cross-training time from 3-weeks down to just 1 day. In some cases it was as low as 30 minutes.

That's not a typo. They reduced cross-training time by more than 95%.

Since agents are now trained to follow digital guides instead of relying on their memory, cross-training simply involves granting them access to a new set of digital guides.

By eliminating the need for extensive memorization in the cross-training process, Find & Follow provides contact centers with a level of flexibility that would otherwise be impossible.

Steps to Scale Up Your Contact Center With Find & Follow

- Run the Find & Follow Workshop.
- Use the Train System to:
  - Create the digital guides, foundational courses, and practice activities
  - Run the training sessions
- Use the Empower System to ensure that agents use the digital guides on every call.
- Use the Adapt System to iron out any problems post-launch.

Chapter 17:

Starting a New Contact Center or Bringing on a BPO Partner

In this chapter, you will learn:
- How three organizations have used Find & Follow to build new contact centers from scratch
- The metrics that were impacted in each organization

Starting a contact center from scratch can be a daunting prospect. Sometimes this may be because of a recent acquisition, a new line of business, or bringing on a new BPO to augment or outsource an existing contact center.

The traditional method is to send out a trainer who is very familiar with the parent company's systems and "train the trainer" in the new contact center so that they can, in turn, train the new supervisors, trainers, and agents.

It is a trainer training a trainer, who will then train a supervisor, who will support a new rep.

If you have ever played the telephone game, then you know how this usually turns out.

There are lots of mistakes, lots of questions, long handle times, lots of stress, and lots of frustration. Most contact centers eventually get over this hurdle, but it takes a long time and is not a pleasant experience.

The Find & Follow Framework can offer several benefits when launching a new contact center or bringing on a BPO partner.

- Decreased time to launch
- Faster time to hit target metrics
- Decreased headcount requirements
- Higher span of control (lower ratio of supervisors to agents)
- Less stress/lower attrition

Customer Story 1

We worked with a client once who had acquired another business. They were taking over the contact center because the previous third-party provider was not hitting their service targets.

Our client wasn't made aware of the project until after the third party had been given notice. They had 120 days to train 30 agents with no supervisors or agents that would have any experience with the product they were supporting. On top of everything, the third-party provider refused to offer any assistance.

The parent company had already worked with our team in some of its other contact centers, so they decided to build a Find & Follow training program right from the beginning.

They divided the hiring groups into three waves. The first wave was trained using a traditional method—a person from the acquired company who had extensive product knowledge lectured them on everything they would need to do. The training took six weeks for Wave 1.

While that was going on, a member of our team recorded all of the lectures, splitting foundational knowledge from actionable knowledge. Digital guides were quickly created for all actionable knowledge. Foundational courses were created for any conceptual or background information the agents would need. Practice activities consisting of real-world scenarios were prepared to help the agents become comfortable following the digital guides.

When Wave 2 was ready to be trained, they didn't sit through any lengthy lectures. They went through foundational courses, were introduced to the digital guides, and then jumped right into the practice activities.

They finished training 50% faster than Wave 1—just three weeks.

Wave 3 finished in just two weeks, with a 66% reduction in training time.

The cutover day came, and the new agents performed like champs. In the first month, they hit service levels of 90% and a quality rate of 98%. As the weeks went on, they continued to improve until their service levels were at 97%.

What They Did to Succeed

- Ran the Find & Follow Workshop
- Listened to existing subject matter experts teach procedures
  - As they listened, they identified and separated actionable and foundational knowledge
- Used the Prepare: Design + Refine System to create the digital guides
- Used the Train System to design the training materials and run the training sessions
- Reviewed each training session and incorporated improvements into the next session in order to drive down training times

Customer Story 2

We worked with another contact center where new hire training took three weeks and time to proficiency took many months. These agents were responsible for scheduling medical appointments for medical offices in several states and had to work from a massive Excel file that contained all the office information.

They transitioned to the Find & Follow Framework for training and supporting agents and cut their training time *and* their time to proficiency down to one week.

They were able to bring on a new third-party BPO to augment their existing team in less than seven days.

What They Did to Succeed

- First, they used the Prepare and Train Systems to drive down the training time for in-house agents.
- Then, they used the same Train System to onboard the BPO to augment their existing team.

Customer Story 3

Another client came to us as they were starting their contact center. The business is a warehouse that serves convenience stores in parts of Texas. At the time, they had a customer service desk where customers could walk up and return items or ask questions. That desk also had to answer the phones.

It was getting to a point where the customer service desk was overwhelmed with the double duty. The business decided that it needed to create a contact center specifically for taking phone calls.

When the business reached out to us, they had no documentation about any processes or procedures. The only thing they had was a written policy for handling returned merchandise.

We applied the Find & Follow principles to create digital guides, foundational courses, and practice activities. We had to create everything from scratch.

After three days of training the Find & Follow way, one of the reps said, "I'd like to hop on the phones and take calls." The next day, another rep said the same thing. By the end of the first week of being in a brand-new contact center, all the newly hired reps were taking calls. By the end of the second week of training, reps took calls during the latter half of the day and were handling them completely on their own.

Within one month, reps were handling the full volume of calls averaging 40 calls/day each, with an SLA of 80% and excellent CSAT scores.

What They Did to Succeed

- Used the Prepare and Train Systems to decrease the training time
- Used the Adapt System to make continual improvements until they hit their target metrics

Summary

- By using the Find & Follow Framework, you can decrease the time it takes to launch a new contact center or bring on a BPO.

Chapter 18:

Losing Key Employees

In this chapter, you will learn:

- How one organization used Find & Follow to decrease their risk of losing crucial company knowledge when key employees leave

Every business fears losing a key employee. But this is especially terrifying for customer service or back-office operations that primarily operate from tribal knowledge.

When all the knowledge about "how things are done" is stuck in people's heads, that knowledge walks right out the door when someone gets promoted or leaves the organization.

Those left behind struggle to piece together their procedures as they look through old emails, try to contact former employees, and dig through computer systems that nobody really understands. This results in terrible customer service, costly mistakes, and extreme stress for everyone involved. Productivity grinds to a halt as supervisors go on a hunting expedition, trying to track down knowledge wherever they can find it.

Sometimes businesses try to solve this problem by forcing employees to document what they do. These employees are rarely trained in how to create usable documentation, so the result is usually just a knowledge dump that is almost completely unusable by anyone but the author. And in most cases, by the time the person leaves, the documentation they created is so out of date that it can only provide clues to those who have to deal with the aftermath of their exit. Things just change too quickly.

So how do you solve this problem?

We had a client that ran into this exact situation. They operated a very complex contact center that had to troubleshoot medical devices over the phone. The backbone of the contact center was made up of agents who had been there a very long time. The agents had a wealth of product knowledge, troubleshooting abilities, and customer experience. But it was all in their heads.

When several of these agents left the organization, the supervisor was stuck. Training new agents was almost impossible. The documentation they did have had never really been used by anyone and didn't simplify anything for the remaining employees.

Everything in the contact center felt very, very hard, and hitting the target service metrics seemed almost impossible.

The contact center leadership worked with us to turn the contact center into a Find & Follow Organization. Digital troubleshooting guides were designed to help new and experienced agents follow a consistent process for troubleshooting the medical devices. Agents were resistant at first, but after, with some determined persistence, they eventually arrived at a state where each agent was handling calls in a consistent manner. Handle times dropped, and their NPS score jumped up by 15 points.

The contact center was no longer beholden to just a few agents who knew everything. The knowledge was centralized. It was shareable, and it was followed by everyone on the team.

But what about the problem of the digital guides getting out of date?

It didn't happen. Why? Because guides that get used get updated. The only real check of whether a digital guide is correct or not is if someone can use it successfully. Things change so fast these days that it is very easy for a software tool, third-party partner, government regulation, or some other unforeseen event to change how a process needs to be followed. But when that guide is used by agents every day, they notice right away when something is out of date. They can then notify the Knowledge Ops Manager, and the guides can be adjusted.

It is never easy to lose a key employee. But when you're operating at the Guide or Train Stage of the Knowledge Ops Maturity Model, you are better prepared to recover quickly when that key employee leaves.

Steps to Decrease the Risk of Losing Key Employees

- Use the Prepare System to:
    - Run the Find & Follow Workshop and identify actionable and foundational knowledge
    - Prepare the digital guides and foundational courses
    - Reward your most knowledgeable employees for using their knowledge to enable others to perform at expert levels.

Summary

When you adopt the Find & Follow Framework, you dramatically decrease the risk of losing institutional knowledge when an employee leaves the organization.

Chapter 19:

Saving a Failing Contact Center

In this chapter, you will learn:

- How Find & Follow can be used to turn around contact centers that are failing to meet basic performance metrics

We had a client come to us once in desperation. They ran a contact center whose service levels were at 30%. That means that they were only answering 30% of their calls within the target time of 30 seconds. And the business was growing, adding new locations and products on a quarterly basis!

One of my favorite clips of all time is the "I Love Lucy Candy Factory" video. You should search for it on YouTube. Lucy and Ethel are assigned to wrap candies that are coming at them on a conveyor belt. Seems simple enough. But slowly, and then quickly, the number of candies starts increasing. Hilarity ensues as Lucy and Ethel try to combat an ever-mounting onslaught of candy that needs to be wrapped.

This is exactly what it can feel like in a contact center that is already overwhelmed but facing increased call volume. But unlike with Lucy and Ethel, nobody is laughing.

You might say, "Why don't they just hire more agents?" But when you are working from tribal knowledge, new hires just exacerbate the problem. They don't know how to do anything, so supervisors who are already maxed out have to slow down to get them up to speed. And when you are working from tribal knowledge, getting up to speed usually takes months, not days.

You end up in a training death spiral where you are drowning under a mountain of calls but are unable to bring more people in to help.

To exit this death spiral, this business decided to implement the Find & Follow training program, allowing them to onboard new agents very quickly and with minimal load on the supervisors.

They followed the following formula:

- Hosted a Find & Follow Workshop to identify situations the agents would need to handle
- Prepared digital guides to guide agents through those situations
- Prepared foundational courses and practice activities to help agents gain confidence using the guides

This contact center hired two new agents. After three days of training, the new agents were handling tickets. After two weeks, the new agents were hitting their target metrics. And after four weeks, the contact center improved its SLA from 30% to 70%.

Summary

Organizations that are floundering can be transformed into highly efficient teams by adopting Find & Follow.

PART VI:

Tips for Launching Find & Follow

"The beginning is the most important part of the work." – Plato

---

We have now covered all the aspects of Find & Follow. In the following chapters, we will give you some suggestions for launching Find & Follow in your organization.

Chapter 20:

Choosing Where to Start

In this chapter, you will learn:

- How to determine where to start your Find & Follow program
- Which strategies have proved ineffective in launching Find & Follow
- The importance of embracing iteration as you launch your Find & Follow program

Launching a Find & Follow program does not have to be an all-or-nothing decision. We find that organizations get the best results when they are very deliberate in the implementation plans, starting with specific teams and then expanding to others.

We have seen three approaches work effectively:

1. A task-focused launch
2. A role-focused launch
3. A department-focused launch

Task-Focused Launch

In a task-focused launch, you focus on creating digital guides for only a handful of situations that have a major impact on performance. Typically, these are complex procedures or troubleshooting situations that are eating up a lot of employee time, causing mistakes, or creating other problems for the business.

By focusing on only the highest impact areas, you can launch your program much more quickly.

This plan only works if you have a few target tasks that have an outsized negative impact on the business because of their complexity.

Role-Focused Launch

In the role-focused launch, instead of focusing on tasks, you focus on all the responsibilities around a specific role. For example, the role of a contact center rep, a junior billing agent, or a bank teller.

Department-Focused Launch

The last option is to launch for all the different roles in a specific department. For example, the entire sales department or the entire customer service department.

> TIPS FROM THE TRENCHES
>
> We suggest using the role-based launch approach. In our experience, it creates the best results. The learnings from launching for one role can quickly be applied as you launch Find & Follow for additional roles.

Launch Approaches We Don't Recommend

Here are some launch strategies that we have found to be less effective:

1. Product-focused launches
2. Software-focused launches

Product-Focused Launches

Clients who have multiple products often want to take a product-focused launch approach. The thinking goes that they can complete all the digital guides for a specific product and then move on to the next one.

That works if you have dedicated teams for each product. But if you have teams that support multiple products, things become confusing because, for Product A, you have digital guides, but for Products B, C, and D, there isn't anything. Employees become unsure as to whether or not they are supposed to use the digital guides or rely on tribal knowledge. The result is that employees are slower to adopt the digital guides, and your culture change takes more time.

A better approach is to do a role-focused approach and cover the 80% of items that are taking up the team's time, regardless of which products they pertain to.

Software-Only Focused Launches

The other big mistake we see is doing an internal software-focused launch. This is very common when launching a new CRM or ERP system. A software-only focused launch will allow you to launch the CRM, ERP, or other systems very quickly, but employees will just as quickly revert back to tribal knowledge after the initial launch.

Why?

Because using software is only one component of their jobs, and they can't use Find & Follow for any of their other tasks. A better strategy is to do a role-based Find & Follow implementation for any roles that will be impacted by the software change.

You can use Find & Follow to launch a CRM, ERP, or other major software systems; just be sure that you don't just limit your digital guides to rudimentary job aids on how to use the software. See the section below for our suggestions on using Find & Follow for major software training.

Launching to Existing Employees

If you are launching a Find & Follow program to existing employees, you probably don't need to create any foundational courses except for one—an overview of and introduction to the digital guides. Your employees probably already understand the concepts around your business and the tools they will need to use. But a short foundational course on how your digital guides will work and why you are going to start using them will help your launch go more smoothly.

Whatever you do, *don't skip the practice activities!*

We have seen organizations that launch their digital guides without having employees go through practice activities. Their launches are never as successful as ones where employees get a chance to practice using the guides to accomplish real tasks. You may be helping them complete activities that they have been doing for a long time, but it is a different experience to use digital guides. Your employees need to take some time to practice using them and increase their confidence.

So, to summarize:

1. Introduce the digital guides to your team.
2. Run practice activities that require them to use the digital guides.

Launching a Training Around a Major Software Rollout (CRM, ERP, etc.)

If you are launching a training around a CRM, ERP, or another major software system, here are some tips for success:

1. Use the Prepare System and the Find & Follow Workshop to identify all the ways the system will impact your employees.
2. Prepare foundational courses that explain why you are making the change, how the employee's job will change, and key concepts around the new software.
3. Prepare digital guides that don't just deal with how to use the software but that guide employees in how to use the software to perform the activities that pertain to their job role.
4. Run practice activities in a sandbox or some other low-impact environment, allowing employees to become comfortable using the digital guides.

Launching a New Hire Training Program

Simply use the Prepare and Train Systems to design your digital guides and training.

Plan to Iterate

Regardless of the launch strategy you choose, you should plan to iterate quickly after you launch. As employees start using your guides, you will receive a lot of feedback. Some things will be unclear. You will discover scenarios that you hadn't anticipated.

Don't worry. This is normal. As you iterate quickly, improving guides and creating new guides to fill in gaps, things will stabilize very quickly.

Summary

- There are several options for starting Find & Follow in your organization:
  - Task-focused
  - Roll-focused
  - Department-focused
  - Product-focused
  - Internal software-focused
- We recommend using a task, roll, or department-focused launch.
- Use a launch strategy that matches your specific needs, whether it be to existing employees, around a new software rollout, or to new hires.
- Plan to iterate quickly as you launch.

Coming up with the plan is usually the easy part. But unless you have buy-in from your entire team, your efforts will get stalled. That is what we are going to cover in the next chapter.

Chapter 21:

Addressing the Fears

In this chapter, you will learn how to address common fears that employees have about Find & Follow, including:

- Fear of change
- Fear of judgment by supervisors
- Fear of becoming redundant

There is a very human element to Find & Follow. The technological changes are just one part of the change. You will be making a major change to the culture that has developed in your organization around sharing and transferring knowledge. This chapter will help you prepare your team for this culture change.

We have already spoken about communicating the vision of what you want to accomplish by using the Knowledge Ops Maturity Model and the Knowledge Ops Flywheel diagrams. But in this chapter, we are going to talk about some common fears you will need to address.

Here are some of the concerns we have heard as we have interviewed supervisors and trainers that have implemented Find & Follow, as well as the employees who have had to change the way they work.

Experienced employees have expressed the following concerns:

- Why do we need this?
- Am I no longer going to be needed once this is launched?
- Our work environment is too complicated. This will never work.
- Why shouldn't new employees have to learn the same way we did?

Less experienced employees have had these concerns:

- Will management look down on me if I need these guides?
- Shouldn't I be trying to learn how to do this without using the guides?
- What will happen if I'm not sure what to do when using a guide?
- Won't following a guide make me sound robotic?

If you don't address these very valid concerns, you may find that despite all your hard work, you don't end up making the progress you had hoped for because your team resists the change.

Fear of Change

We had one client who used an approach that was very successful. They were working with multiple senior managers, some of whom had been working in the organization for almost 20 years. They had some pretty entrenched work habits, and Find & Follow was going to be a major shift.

The supervisor gathered everyone in a room and explained how things were going to change. They weren't going to use PDF guides anymore. They weren't going to be allowed to print out cheat sheets anymore. They were going to be expected to use the digital guides on every call.

She then gave them a moment and just asked them how those changes made them feel. Some of the team leads brought up concerns. Some wondered if the guides would really work, so they brought up several digital guides and had the senior managers go through them. They did this all in a private meeting with just the senior managers, allowing that group to work through their initial reactions without their direct reports around them.

Someone said, "So we really can't use our cheat sheets anymore?" The supervisor responded, "Yes, why do you think that is?"

"Oh, it's probably because things are always changing, and these printed copies get out of date really quickly."

The supervisor gave the team leads time to process things. She showed them how they would be contributing to improving the effectiveness of the digital guides. She also explained that this wasn't going to be perfect at first, and it never would be. That was why they needed the contribution of everyone to continually improve the system.

Fear of Judgment by Supervisors

Another group that was working with all new hires didn't face any initial resistance. Since it was a brand-new contact center, no one had any preconceived notions about how they had done work there before. They launched with amazing performance numbers, but after a few weeks, their performance started to drop. Looking at the analytics, we could tell that they weren't using the digital guides as often as they had previously. They had started relying on their memories.

Jonathan from our team received permission from the client to interview several of their agents to understand what was going on. While these agents were new to this contact center, they had experience working in other contact centers. In those previous work environments, relying on documentation had been seen as a crutch. Agents were expected to commit everything to memory if they wanted to impress their supervisors. They thought that their supervisors at the current contact center expected the same from them.

Once we learned this, the supervisors went back and told the agents that they would never be penalized or looked down upon for using the digital guides. In fact, it was quite the opposite. They were *expected* to use the digital guides on every call.

The performance numbers quickly went back up.

Fear of Becoming Redundant

One of the biggest concerns longtime employees have is that they will eventually be replaced by the digital guides. Every organization has a few people that have all the experience and knowledge that is needed to keep the business running. While being the only person that has all the answers can be a huge burden, it also provides quite a bit of job security. Some employees believe that if all the knowledge in their heads is captured in a digital guide, then they will be seen as redundant, and their position will be eliminated.

That is possible, but in our experience, that usually isn't the way things play out. If these very experienced employees engage in the Find & Follow process, they all of a sudden start creating much more value for the organization instead of being a knowledge bottleneck that slows everything down. They no longer do everything, but they help everyone else do more.

The reality is that businesses change operations all the time. In some cases, that leads to more hiring, and in some cases, it results in people being let go. But with some willingness to change, these experienced employees can successfully use their wealth of knowledge to move into the role of a Knowledge Champion.

> **Summary**
>
> To change your tribal knowledge culture and become a Find & Follow Organization, you will need to address fears that your team may have about the changes in behaviors and expectations. These include:
>
> - Fear of change
> - Fear of judgment by supervisors
> - Fear of becoming redundant

Now that we have addressed these fears, let's look at a best practice for launching Find & Follow quickly in your team—the 80% Launch.

Chapter 22:

Doing an 80% Launch

In this chapter, you will learn:

- What an 80% Launch is
- Why it is so effective
- How to design and perform an 80% Launch

What Is an 80% Launch?

The 80% Launch approach helps you launch an effective Find & Follow program as quickly as possible.

An 80% Launch means you have guides for the procedures that take up to 80% of your employees' time. It doesn't mean that if you list 100 total digital guides that could be created, you must create 80 of them before you launch your guides. It means that if of those 100 digital guides, about 30 of them would address 80% of the activities that employees do on a regular basis, then create those 30 guides and launch.

How Did We Land on 80%?

It strikes the right balance between launching your program quickly and ensuring you have enough content to make an impact on employee performance when you launch.

Creating content for the activities that take up 80% of your employees' time is much more achievable than covering 100% of all the scenarios they might encounter.

If your employees can find what they need in your digital guides 80% of the time, their performance will improve, and the burden on your supervisors will decrease.

The content that covers the additional 20% (which you will create after launching your Find & Follow program) deals with procedures that your employees don't frequently use. They have a lesser impact on your operations.

How to Do an 80% Launch

1. Identify the activities that cause 80% of the problems.

Using your Find & Follow Report from the workshop, identify which activities cause 80% of the problems.

You can look at this in two ways:

1. Which tasks are they required to perform 80% of the time?
2. Which tasks, when they come up, cause the biggest problems (questions, mistakes, etc.)?

It really depends on your work environment. If your team is able to perform their normal day-to-day tasks without too much help, then target the most complicated scenarios first.

If your team struggles in their day-to-day tasks, then target the most frequently performed tasks first.

Either way, you want to tackle the tasks that are causing 80% of the problems (questions, mistakes, etc.). This could be 10 tasks, 20 tasks, or 100 tasks. Whatever the number, if you create digital guides for those tasks, things will improve significantly.

This list will be much more manageable than trying to complete everything, and it will have a tremendous impact on productivity.

2. Determine when you will launch.

Choose a launch date. You'll want to be realistic about this target date. This will depend on how many articles you need to create.

Then set deadlines leading up to the launch date for creating and testing the content.

> TIPS FROM THE TRENCHES
>
> We've launched a client in as little as two weeks because we already had a lot of content, and the worksheet helped us identify the top 80% of activities that employees needed to perform. After launching, there was still work to be done. But since employees could reference the digital guides instead of their supervisor, their supervisor was able to dedicate more time to creating guides.

3. Identify existing content.

You probably already have some content lying around. It could be in emails, chat messages, Word documents, etc. Decide which content you can use and improve.

4. Fill in the gaps and improve the content.

You will probably find that there are many gaps in your content or that your existing content isn't findable, followable, or scannable. That is all right. Just use the principles in the Prepare: Design + Refine System to fill in gaps or make your existing content findable, followable, and scannable.

5. Backfill content after launch.

After you launch your Find & Follow Training and things have stabilized a bit, start backfilling your digital guides.

One suggestion is to create empty digital guides for activities that weren't included in the 80% Launch that simply say, "Contact a supervisor for assistance." Then when those situations come up after your launch, supervisors or Knowledge Champions will know exactly where to add the required guide. You will also prevent your employees from searching for a digital guide that doesn't exist yet.

> **Summary**
>
> - The 80% Launch will help you launch more quickly while still making a big impact.
> - To do an 80% Launch, do the following:
>   - Identify the activities that cause 80% of the problems.
>   - Identify a launch date.
>   - Identify existing content.
>   - Fill in the gaps.
>   - Backfill content post-launch.

In the next chapter, we are going to talk about ideas for optimizing your operations post-launch.

Chapter 23:

Optimizing Your Knowledge Operations After Launching Find & Follow

In this chapter, you will learn how to optimize your operations after your Find & Follow launch, including:

- How to use search reports
- How to triage comments
- How to find new opportunities for improvements
- How to review content to ensure it stays accurate
- How to ensure you use the Adapt System to manage change

In the business world, we tend to focus on projects and launching. Once something is released, we step away and move on to the next thing. But that's like planting a garden and walking away only to let the weeds take over and ruin our hard work.

Find & Follow is not something you launch and then walk away from. It's an ongoing effort to maintain and optimize digital guides so that your organization can continue to experience value.

There are several activities that your knowledge ops team will need to engage in:

1. Analyze Search Reports
2. Triage Comments
3. Find New Opportunities
4. Review Content for Accuracy
5. Ensure Application of the Empower and Adapt Systems

Analyze Search Reports

Search reports are reports that will show you what terms employees are searching on and which articles they are clicking on. Using these reports, your knowledge ops team can:

- Identify articles that need to be created. If they see search requests that are returning empty results, it is a good sign that there is some content missing from the knowledge base.
- Identify articles that need additional search terms. Sometimes you will see search phrases where you know what the employee is looking for, but they aren't getting any results because they have used a different term than that which was used in the digital guide. This is a great time to go back to the guide and add meta-search terms so that the digital guide will show up for the alternate phrase.

Using search reports will allow your knowledge ops team to be proactive instead of just reactive.

Triage Comments

As your employees use your digital guides, they will often notice changes that need to be made or recognize new articles that need to be created. Your knowledge base should have a function that allows employees to leave feedback on the guides to inform your knowledge ops team that things are outdated or inaccurate.

The knowledge ops team should triage these comments, updating or creating articles right away when necessary.

Comments do not need to be published back to the article. You never want your "knowledge" to be in the comments. All the pertinent information should be incorporated into the official digital guide. The comment can then be deleted or archived.

Find New Opportunities

The knowledge ops team can also look for new opportunities to empower more productivity. Once you move beyond the obvious procedures, there are many other areas where checklists and decision trees can improve your organization's productivity. Here are just a few examples:

- Do you have weekly, monthly, or quarterly meetings? Create preparation checklists for all people involved.
- Do you have regular decisions that need to be made? Make a list of items that should be considered each time that type of decision needs to be made. Or build in some logic to a decision tree that will help clarify the best way forward.
- Do you perform regular interviews with job applicants? Make a bulleted list of key questions that you want to ask.
- Are you trying to instill a new sales methodology for your team? Create a pre and post-call checklist for them to review.

In none of these cases are we replacing the actual thinking that needs to go on. We are just offloading as much memorization as possible so that employees' minds are free to focus on what matters most in their roles.

You can also look for opportunities by speaking with managers and executives about performance issues and metrics that are going in the wrong direction. Maybe there's been an uptick in overtime, or field agents are being sent to locations to fix products that weren't actually broken.

With a little thought, you will find opportunities everywhere in your business to increase your team's productivity by helping them do tasks more consistently and relying less and less on their memories.

Review Content for Accuracy

If your digital guides are being used on a regular basis, then they'll naturally remain up to date because employees will leave comments when they see inaccuracies. But some digital guides are only used once a quarter or once a year. Those are harder to keep up to date because nobody is reminding you to check them out.

Come up with a system or use a knowledge base that has a feature to periodically remind you to review your digital guides and sign off on them.

Ensure Application of the Empower and Adapt Systems

We have mentioned this before, but your knowledge ops team will need to ensure that everyone is implementing the Empower and Adapt Systems of the Find & Follow Framework. The Knowledge Champion may need to review the principles of these systems with supervisors, coaches, and trainers to ensure that the team doesn't slide back into old tribal knowledge habits.

> **Summary**
>
> The knowledge ops team, and especially the Knowledge Champion, will be able to find opportunities to further optimize employee performance. They can do this by:
>
> - Analyzing search reports
> - Triaging comments and updating digital guides
> - Finding new opportunities for improvement
> - Reviewing content for accuracy
> - Ensuring that teams are applying the Empower and Adapt Systems as they support employees

We have now covered everything you need to know about the Find & Follow Framework. You never need to rely on tribal knowledge again!

Part VII:

Summing Up

"Give a man a fish, and you feed him for a day; teach a man to fish, and you feed him for a lifetime." – Maimonides

---

Chapter 24:

Confidence, Consistency, and Independence

Can you imagine driving across the United States without a GPS? Can you imagine cooking a new meal every day without being able to reference a recipe?

For too long, that is how our businesses and organizations have operated. We have relied on PowerPoints, word of mouth, shadowing, and Slack messages to cram more and more information into the limited capacities of our memories. This has led to horrendous customer service, expensive mistakes, and stressed-out organizations.

It doesn't have to be this way. I spoke with an operations director for a contact center at a public utility who had been through the Find & Follow transformation. Here is how she described the experience:

It's been fascinating to watch. Everything you guys said would happen has absolutely happened. Even our employees, who we thought would just dig their heels in and refuse to change, even they are saying, "This is so great! I have everything at my fingertips!" But so does everybody else. And now we have that consistency of how to do the steps.

So it's been fun to be able to see this because they already knew how to do things, right? These are seasoned employees. But they were skipping steps before. So it's getting them to slow down. The first one that they process is kind of a disaster because they're trying to jump ahead, and they're nervous, but then once they actually slow down and take the time and read the information, it actually goes much faster. They don't realize it, but it goes much faster.

And there's more accuracy to it. They can handle procedures that they have never seen before. They can complete tasks where they used to get stuck.

It was interesting because one of the employees actually had written on a piece of paper that when a situation came up, she needed to escalate the call to a supervisor. She was just about to do that even with ScreenSteps. I said, oh, no, girl. No, you're doing this; you're doing the whole article. And she was able to do it! So with something that she had previously handed off, she was just able to follow the steps and do the things. Which is amazing, right? It's everything we hoped it would be. And to actually see it coming to life is amazing.

I can't thank you guys enough. It's just everything you said it would be. Not that I ever doubted you. But if we can transform this team, then we can do it anywhere. At first, I thought, "Oh, Greg doesn't understand our situation. They don't know how hard it is here." But now I see that it can happen anywhere.

For a new hire to be able to get to the point where they could really process a move-in or move-out in our old training style, it would have taken six months. This was week four for them. And they're processing move-ins already, which means they feel like they're contributing. Everybody else on the floor is like, wow, they've only been here four weeks, and they're already *directly making our lives easier. So it's been absolutely just transformative. It is amazing.*

All they did was change the way they thought about knowledge transfer. Knowledge wasn't something you had to cram in your head. It was something you could find and follow right when you needed it.

If you want to get started in your journey, take these steps:

- Review the Knowledge Ops Maturity Model. Be honest about where you are and where you want to be.
- Start implementing the Find & Follow Framework, moving one team at a time up to the Guide or Train Stage.
- Embrace a new way of using knowledge at work.
- Continue to iterate, optimize, and improve.

And if you need some additional guidance, get in touch. We would love to help you on your journey to helping your employees do more with less stress in less time.

Appendix:

Best Practices and Tips

In this section, we will detail best practices and tips for the various aspects of the Find & Follow Framework that we have covered in previous chapters.

Knowledge Champions and Knowledge Ops Managers

If you are launching Find & Follow for a single team, you may only need a Knowledge Champion. The Knowledge Champion's primary responsibility is to ensure that knowledge is designed in a way that employees can find and follow it, empowering those employees to perform their job effectively.

A Knowledge Champion is in charge of the following as it pertains to their team:

1. **Identify learning gaps:** The Knowledge Champion identifies gaps in the existing content and observes where employees are struggling or confused. Feedback from employees and direct observation can help identify these gaps. They will primarily use Find & Follow Workshops (described in an earlier chapter) to identify these gaps.
2. **Identify experts:** The Knowledge Champion establishes relationships with department leaders and experts in various fields within the company. These experts can provide advice and information to fill the knowledge gaps.

3. **Extract knowledge from experts:** The Knowledge Champion gathers information and knowledge from the experts either by having them write articles themselves or through interviews conducted by the Knowledge Champion or the knowledge authoring team.
4. **Write, refine, and publish content:** Based on the information gathered, the Knowledge Champion or the expert writes the content. The Knowledge Champion reviews and edits the content for accuracy and clarity, ensuring it is easy to follow.
5. **Ensure digital guides are incorporated in new hire training:** The Knowledge Champion works with trainers and supervisors to integrate digital guides into new hire training programs.
6. **Communicate changes with the team:** The Knowledge Champion informs the team about new articles or updates to existing ones. This ensures that employees are aware of the changes and the importance of using the knowledge base for their tasks.
7. **Monitor the use of the knowledge base:** The Knowledge Champion tracks the usage of the knowledge base using analytics tools. This helps identify which articles are most viewed, how frequently they are accessed, and which keywords are commonly used. The data gathered can be used to make improvements and address any learning gaps.

The Knowledge Champion keeps the wheels of information spinning, ensuring that employees have all the information they need at their fingertips.

Skills

Here are some required skills for the Knowledge Champion role:

- Ability to write clearly and concisely
- Critical thinking and problem-solving
- Empathy
- Ability to design digital guides that logically guide others through complex processes
- Ability to interview others to discover role requirements
- Highly organized
- Comfortable with technology
- A strong desire to empower employees to be able to work independently

Knowledge Operations Manager

If you are implementing Find & Follow in a larger organization and across multiple teams, you may want to introduce the role of Knowledge Operations Manager. This role oversees the Knowledge Champions on each team, ensuring efficiency and consistency across the team.

Responsibilities

- Communicate the Find & Follow vision to all stakeholders
- Train and support Knowledge Champions in their responsibilities
- Support Knowledge Champions and supervisors in helping employees rely on digital guides instead of tribal knowledge
- Assist in running Find & Follow Workshops
- Establish style guides and best practices for all Knowledge Champions
- Manage overall knowledge base health across multiple teams

Skills

- All of the same skills as a Knowledge Champion
- Strong leadership skills
- Ideally, experience driving change within organizations
- A strong desire to empower employees to be able to work independently

The Knowledge Ops Manager is the leader of the knowledge ops team. They can work with the Knowledge Champion to coach them on best practices, help them design a new hire training program, or prepare for a significant transformational change, but the bulk of the day-to-day maintenance of content for their team will be done by the Knowledge Champion.

The Knowledge Ops Manager helps everyone in the organization abandon old tribal knowledge habits and move to the higher stages of the Knowledge Ops Maturity Model.

Organizing the Knowledge Ops Team

If you have both Knowledge Ops Managers and Knowledge Champions, your people may be organized as follows:

- Knowledge Ops Team
  - Knowledge Ops Manager
  - Finance
    - Knowledge Champion for Finance
  - HR
    - Knowledge Champion for HR
  - Customer Service
    - Knowledge Champion for Customer Service

This doesn't mean that you need to go out and hire a bunch of new people. The Knowledge Champion for each team can be the supervisor who previously was in charge of answering employee questions and fixing their mistakes. You are just going to shift the way they spend their time from constantly putting out fires to preventing those fires from ever starting.

Instead of constantly responding to emails and chats (spending), they will be creating, updating, and refining reusable digital guides (investing).

Running the Find & Follow Workshop

Where Should You Host the Workshop?

We have run workshops in person or remotely. Both work equally well, but you need a few things.

Tips for running the workshop in person:

1. Get a whiteboard. This will make diagramming things so much easier.
2. Have somebody taking notes in a spreadsheet or other document.
3. Use a projector or TV. As you are capturing information, you want to make sure that everyone can see and comment on what you have captured.

Tips for running the workshop virtually:

1. Cameras on. No exceptions. You need to see what people are thinking and how they are reacting. Video is crucial.
2. Use an online whiteboarding tool. We use Miro and have found that to work very well.
3. Ask somebody to capture notes.

Running the Workshop

Get ready for a lively discussion! We find that most organizations haven't analyzed what an employee in a specific role needs to be able to do in their job to this degree. This process will add a lot of clarity for the whole team (and make everyone appreciate what someone in the target role really needs to be able to do).

Ask everyone to come prepared by reviewing what employees do on a daily basis. If you're doing a workshop for customer service, review the last 150 service tickets to get ideas on what types of requests agents receive. If you have actual data such as request types, error rates, escalations, etc., that is even better.

Setting the Ground Rules

Without some concerted effort on the part of the facilitator, these workshops can quickly go down rabbit holes and get diverted on interesting but unnecessary tangents.

To prevent this, you want to set some ground rules:

1. You are just going to discuss the target role. You will save discussions of other roles in the organization for another workshop.
2. You are only going to discuss how things actually are, not how they should be.
3. You will all feel free to disagree with each other but be respectful in your disagreement.
4. You will put discussions that get too into the weeds into a "parking lot" to be revisited later. At this stage, you want to get the names of the tasks that need to be done and a general idea of the sub-tasks and variables, but you are not writing the digital guides during this meeting.

Rule #2 is the hardest to follow. Once you start analyzing all that an employee in the target role needs to be able to do, you will see opportunities for improvement everywhere. That is wonderful. Capture those ideas for a future discussion, but don't take the time to discuss them now.

Optimization discussions can go on forever and will divert you from the task at hand. We always enforce a strict "No optimization" rule in our workshops. We have to deal with the messy reality of how things work today, not how they will work in some ideal future state.

Additional Tips for Identifying Activities

You would think that this part is pretty simple, but we have found that teams often get stuck when trying to generate the list of activities. Here are a few tips that will help you identify every activity that pertains to the target job role.

Tip #1: Build Out Topic Areas

Build out a list of topic areas. The topic areas you use will be specific to your business and the target job role. Here are some examples that you could use to generate your topic areas:

- Software applications that the employee will use
- Types of transactions they need to complete
- Reason codes that you use in your customer service software
- Customer segments that they will support

Once again, the purpose is not to have everything perfectly categorized. The purpose of the topic areas is to make sure you have identified as many activities as possible.

Tip #2: Use Frequency of Activities

To help spur more ideas, list activities that happen on a daily, weekly, monthly, quarterly, annual, or random basis.

Handling Disagreements

The first part of the workshop is going to be quite messy. People will disagree about what needs to be accomplished or how it needs to be done. They will disagree about who is responsible for doing something.

That's all right. It is all part of the purpose and the process. As you talk through each activity, identifying who is responsible and what the variables are, you will create clarity for everyone around this job role.

You will probably discover that there are many decisions that have never actually been made in the business—things have just evolved and happened. That is OK as well. Try to capture what your team actually does as closely as possible. There will be opportunities to optimize and refine policies and procedures later on.

Building Digital Guides That Can Stand Alone

Moving Beyond the Clicks

Find & Follow is not concerned with just helping employees click on the right buttons. It is not simply a job aid that gives you a quick tutorial on a piece of software.

Find & Follow accounts for your policies, procedures, troubleshooting, and tools to ensure that employees can do what they need to do and in the way they are supposed to do it. It encompasses the entire context in which the employee works.

A Find & Follow Organization will focus on helping employees do the following:

1. Respond to requests
2. Answer questions
3. Complete tasks
4. Make decisions
5. Solve problems

When employees can do these five things correctly, they are able to work independently and efficiently.

An Online Searchable Knowledge Base (or Knowledge Ops Platform)

Word, PDF, and Excel files are not going to cut it anymore. Your team will need a searchable knowledge base or knowledge operations platform that contains digital articles and not just file attachments.

A knowledge base is a centralized location where your team can search for and find online documentation. These articles will typically contain text, images, or even video. A knowledge base is primarily for capturing information and making it searchable.

A knowledge ops platform is like a knowledge base but with additional capabilities that allow you to apply all four systems in the Find & Follow Framework (Prepare, Train, Empower, and Adapt). If you would like to see an example of what a knowledge ops platform can do, go to www.screensteps.com.

A knowledge ops platform will help you create digital guides that are more effective than standard knowledge base articles, word files, or recorded videos.

These digital guides will allow you to:

- Gradually reveal information to the employee as needed
- Handle long and/or complex procedures
- Iterate quickly as you optimize your digital guides
- Update content swiftly as things change

The standard tools of knowledge management and e-learning won't help employees perform all these activities. When we look at an organization's knowledge resources, they typically consist of the following:

- Word, Excel, PDF, and PowerPoint files
- Videos
- Flowcharts
- Job aids

While Find & Follow can leverage these resources, the primary tools used in Find & Follow are as follows:

- Standard articles: For short how-to guides or reference information
- Interactive checklists: For lengthier processes that follow a single path
- Decision trees: For procedures that can follow multiple paths

Let's look at some example situations and compare how they would traditionally be handled versus how they would be handled from a Find & Follow perspective.

Situation	Traditional Documentation Resources	Find & Follow Resources
Customer calls in and asks to return a product.	Word document on the return policy PDF job aid on processing a return	Decision tree that guides the employee through the process of determining if the product can be returned Decision tree that guides the employee through the steps of processing the return, making sure to account for all the variables
Customer asks why their water bill is so high.	Lengthy Word files explaining how to investigate the reason for the high water bill	An interactive checklist that lists the areas to investigate Each checklist item can be expanded to reveal more detail for less experienced employees
Employee needs to update their availability in the work management system.	PDF job aid with text and some images	Searchable article with detailed screenshots
An employee has to decide whether or not a price increase should be charged to a customer.	Word document that explains the policy	Decision tree that guides the employee in applying the price increase policy
An employee needs to troubleshoot why a customer is not seeing report data.	Multi-page Word file with troubleshooting information	Decision tree that guides the employee through the most efficient process of troubleshooting the problem

The biggest difference between the traditional resources and the Find & Follow resources is that the Find & Follow resources are designed to be used "in the moment."

What standard do these guides need to meet? The digital guide should be designed in such a way that if I were on the phone with a customer, I would be able to find and follow it without having to put the customer on hold or making them wait while I read instructions.

Let's dive into these tools in a little more detail.

The Interactive Checklist

If you haven't read *The Checklist Manifesto* by Atul Gawande, then you should. He clearly makes a case for the effectiveness of checklists in highly complex work environments, such as hospitals, airplanes, and manufacturing. Checklists are a very simple tool that increases productivity and reduces mistakes.

But checklists have to perform a balancing act. Experienced employees just want the bare necessities in the checklist because that makes the checklist easier to use. Less experienced employees need more detailed instructions on how to complete each step.

Atul Gawande explains, "It is common to misconceive how checklists function in complex lines of work. They are not comprehensive how-to guides, whether for building a skyscraper or getting a plane out of trouble. They are quick and simple tools aimed to buttress the skills of expert professionals."[8]

So what are less-experienced employees supposed to do if checklists are only for "expert professionals"?

---

[8] Gawande, Atul. *The Checklist Manifesto: How to Get Things Right.* Henry Holt and Co. Kindle Edition, p. 128.

We need a solution that can serve both audiences, and the answer is the interactive checklist. Interactive checklists appear as a standard checklist but allow less experienced employees to click on any checklist item to see detailed instructions.

This keeps the checklist to a reasonable length, prevents experienced employees from seeing detail that they don't need, and allows less experienced employees to quickly access additional detail as needed.

Scan this QR code below to see an example of an interactive checklist.

www.screensteps.com/find-follow-book/resources/interactive-checklists

The Decision Tree

Decision trees make it simpler to follow complex procedures. Decision trees will greatly simplify your digital guides if your procedures are filled with "if ... then" statements.

A decision tree asks an employee questions and then gives them step-by-step guidance based on their answers. It is like having a digital coach that talks you through a complex procedure.

A standard article might look something like this:

Process for Changing an Account Owner for a Software Business Application

Sometimes customers need to change the owner on their account. If the current owner contacts us, then we can switch the owner to another user on the account. If the current owner is no longer working at the customer's business, then we will need to verify the change some other way. First, check to see if the person contacting you is already an admin user on the account. Etc.

This can be greatly simplified if we translate it into a decision tree.

Decision trees are difficult to represent in a printed book, so I suggest you visit the link below to see a full example.

Scan this QR code to see an interactive example of this decision tree.

www.screensteps.com/find-follow-book/resources/decision-trees

---

Here is a non-interactive version that will hopefully give you some idea of how they are structured.

> **DECISION TREE FOR CHANGING AN ACCOUNT OWNER FOR A SOFTWARE BUSINESS APPLICATION**
>
> Are you speaking to the current account owner?
> - Yes
>   - Change the owner to be whomever they designate.
> - No
>   - Verify that the person contacting you is an admin user on the account.
>   - Are they an admin user?
>   - Yes
>   - Etc.
>   - No
>   - Etc.

Decision trees can make it much easier to follow complex procedures or policies.

Decision trees also reduce the cognitive load on an employee who is trying to follow a guide. Instead of reading detailed instructions and then struggling to adapt those instructions to their current situation, the employee simply answers questions and follows the step-by-step guidance.

Decision trees are ideal for helping employees know how to troubleshoot problems, navigate complex procedures, or correctly apply company policies.

The Standard Article

The final tool is the standard article. This can be used for short job aids, straightforward procedures, reference information, or FAQs. The important thing to note is that this is an article, not an encyclopedia. The most common mistake we see businesses make is cramming too much information into one document. It is not uncommon to see PDFs that are 50, 100, or even 500 pages long. Standard articles should be much shorter than this and should generally answer one question, not 20 to 30.

For example, a standard article might be titled "How to Update an Invoice With a PO#," and it will be three or four screenshots and a little text walking through the clicks. That's it.

Another standard article might be titled "Wire Transfer Information," and it will consist of a short, bulleted list that only includes information required to perform a wire transfer.

Determining Which Tool to Use

It's very tempting when you get a new hammer to look at everything as a nail. The same is true in knowledge operations. We especially see this problem with decision trees. For most organizations, decision trees are a relatively new and exciting tool, so they instantly start using them everywhere, even in places where an interactive checklist or standard article would be better.

Using a standard article in a situation that really requires a decision tree is like trying to dig a 6' pit with a tablespoon. And using a decision tree when a simple bulleted list would work is like using a sledgehammer to pound in a nail.

Choosing the right tool for the situation makes all the difference when trying to turn knowledge into performance.

Here are some simple tips for writing articles. Imagine someone asking you, "How do I ..."?

If your answer is, "It depends," then use a decision tree.

If your answer is "Click here, then click there," then use a standard article with screenshots.

If your answer is, "You have to do several things," then use an interactive checklist.

These questions won't cover every case, but they should give you a good idea of which tool would be appropriate for your given situation.

Organizing Your Guides

This is an area we see a lot of people getting tripped up. In most cases, we see people making this more complicated than it needs to be.

The general rule of thumb is to organize your digital guides in an intuitive way that matches how things are generally organized in your business.

If you're creating digital guides for your entire company, then we recommend organizing your digital guides by department and role (e.g., Sales, Marketing, Billing). That way, an employee can go directly to all the digital guides that they will need to use. If you have some guides that are shared across roles, you can organize them into folders grouped by software application or topic.

If you're creating digital guides for a specific role or department, then you can organize your digital guides by topic or work area (e.g., Invoices, Purchase Orders, Payroll, Insurance).

Since your employees will mostly search for your guides, I would suggest not getting too hung up on the folder structure. Most modern knowledge bases will let you reorganize your article structure pretty easily, so starting with department and role will help you get started quickly without overthinking things.

5 Principles for Preparing Digital Courses

Here are five principles to follow as you build out your foundational courses:

1. Use context to increase comfort.
2. Help employees become familiar with the neighborhood.
3. Let the digital guides do their work.
4. Add links to the digital guides they will use.
5. Limit the time.

Use Context to Increase Comfort

The primary purpose of the foundational courses is to help employees understand the environment they will be working in.

Let's say that I work in the billing department of an organization. I get asked to generate a quote for 34 widgets. There is a guide called "How to Prepare a Quote" that is going to help me complete that task.

But I will feel much more comfortable and confident following that guide if I understand some background concepts first.

- What products do we sell?
- Who will ask for a quote?
- What will they do with the quote?
- What is the purchase process customers typically go through to buy something from us?

None of that information belongs in the digital guide. It should be covered in a foundational course with the expectation that this general information will be internalized by the employee. By helping employees internalize some of the contexts around their work, we increase the employee's level of comfort with the digital guides.

Help Employees Become Familiar With the Neighborhood

Another principle is to help them become familiar with the neighborhood they will be working in. What is the neighborhood?

- The software or other tools they will use on a regular basis
- The people they will interact with

You don't need to go into too much detail here, especially in regard to the software. Just introduce them to the software tools they will be using, provide a brief overview and general navigation, and communicate how the different software tools will fit together.

Let the Digital Guides Do Their Work

It is crucial that you let the digital guides do their work. Too many trainers prepare their training materials as if their digital guides didn't exist. You really shouldn't be teaching anything in your foundational courses that are covered in your digital guides.

Your digital guides are going to answer the question, "How do I …?"

Don't repeat those answers in your foundational courses.

Why wouldn't you want to teach the "How do I …?" information? Because your employees don't have a chance of remembering all the details. That is why the digital guides are there. The digital guides will do the remembering for them.

Add Links to the Digital Guides They Will Use

You introduce your employee to the digital guides they will use by adding links to them in your foundational courses. You should not expect your employees to review the digital guides or memorize them. You are just presenting the guides to them so that they get a sense of what support they will have when they actually start completing real tasks.

Limit the Time

Foundational courses should be short. We recommend staying right around 20 minutes with a max time of 30 minutes.

What do you do if you need to cover more material than will fit in 20 minutes? Break your material up into multiple foundational courses. Depending on the complexity of your business, you will have a different number of courses.

We recently helped a chain of car washes launch a Find & Follow Training for their contact center. They had six foundational courses. In contrast, we also worked with a medical insurance provider. They had 26 foundational courses.

Balance Scope and Detail

If you aren't sure how to break up your courses, think about the relationship between scope and detail.

The scope of your course is how much information you are going to cover.

The detail is how granular you will get with your information.

If we have a 20-minute time limit, we can adjust our scope and detail to fit within that time. Our first course may cover the overall operations of the business. That would be considered a large scope. If we have a large scope, we will have very shallow detail.

But what if we need a course that has more detail in it? No problem, we will just decrease the scope.

By adjusting scope and detail in your courses, you can keep them short and focused. You can almost think of them as building blocks. Longer, shorter blocks have high scope and low detail. They lay a foundation that later courses can build on with lower scope and more detail.

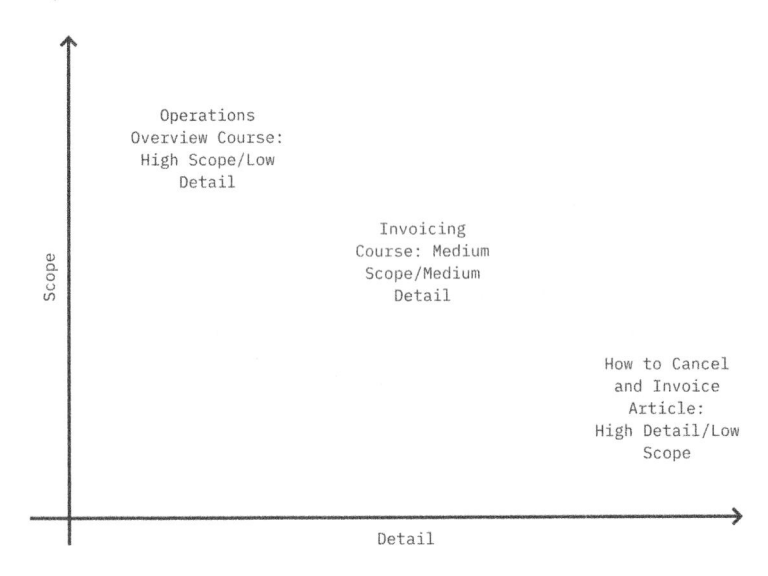

```
       ▲
       │
       │    Operations
       │    Overview Course:
       │    High Scope/Low
       │        Detail
       │
       │                    Invoicing
       │                 Course: Medium
 Scope │                 Scope/Medium
       │                      Detail
       │
       │                                How to Cancel
       │                                 and Invoice
       │                                   Article:
       │                                High Detail/Low
       │                                     Scope
       │
       └──────────────────────────────────────────────▶
                            Detail
```

Preparing Practice Activities

Tips for Creating Practice Activities
Here are some tips for creating your practice activities:

- Start with easy scenarios.
- Build up to more complex scenarios.
- Make sure you cover a variety of situations.

Start With Easy Scenarios
We have seen trainers that instantly go to the most complicated scenario they can think of when training a new employee. When asked why they are doing this, they respond, "Well, that is what it is really like," or "We need to humble them a bit."

Those responses are misguided.

The purpose of practice activities is to increase the employee's confidence in working independently. You don't increase confidence by starting out with the hardest scenario first.

Build up to More Complex Scenarios
Other trainers make the mistake of *only* dealing with simple or ideal scenarios. When this happens, employees leave training underprepared to deal with real-world situations. You don't want

to start too hard, but you eventually want to get to scenarios that match the complexity of the actual situations the employee will need to respond to.

Make Sure You Cover a Variety of Situations

You don't need to cover every variation of every scenario. But you do want to make sure that you cover a variety of scenarios. The primary purpose of having a wide variety is to increase the employee's confidence that the digital guides will be able to guide them through a variety of situations.

Running Training Sessions

Remote Training

Find & Follow works wonderfully for remote training. In most remote training, employees are bored and disengaged. In Find & Follow Training, everyone is active and learning. Here are some tips for running a Find & Follow Training remotely:

- If you have video recordings of your courses, let employees watch them individually. Some employees may want to take some extra time to review specific sections. That is fine. But let everyone go at their own pace.
- Engage everyone in the practice activities. After you complete an activity with a single employee, ask for comments and observations from others.
- If you have enough new hires, split up into breakout rooms and have the new hires run practice activities for each other. Just make sure that you provide the employees with scripts for the practice activities.

If your team is used to running long PowerPoint presentations or lectures over Zoom, they are going to *love* Find &

Follow Training. They will be engaged in learning right from the beginning. And because they have to actually *do* things during the training, you never have to worry about employees zoning out.

Things That Can Sabotage Your Training Sessions

Running a Find & Follow Training session can be a big shift for experienced trainers. They're used to delivering lectures, teaching students, answering questions, and working really hard to make sure that their training sessions are entertaining and engaging. A Find & Follow session is a very different experience for a trainer. And if trainers continue to do the same things they have always done, they can actually sabotage your Find & Follow training efforts.

Here are a few red flags to look for.

Trainers That Won't Stop Lecturing

Nobody likes to admit this, but many of us who train like to hear ourselves speak. Trainers need to rely on the foundational course materials and digital guides.

Being a facilitator is much different than being a lecturer, and it takes a bit of practice. A Find & Follow trainer has to be committed to empowering employees to work independently, not just trying to fill their heads with information.

Trainers need to become the guide on the side instead of the sage on the stage.

Trainers That Answer Questions or Fill in Knowledge Gaps

This may seem counterintuitive. Shouldn't trainers be answering the questions employees have? Isn't that how they will learn?

It depends on the question being asked. If an employee is asking "how" to do something, then the trainer needs to encourage them to follow the digital guides. If the guide is incorrect or unclear, then the guide needs to be updated.

We had one group of trainers who told us that they wanted to create a friendly atmosphere where everyone felt comfortable during training, so they needed to answer employee questions.

Guess what happened—the employees weren't able to work independently after training. The employees may have felt very comfortable during training, but they felt very uncomfortable later on when they weren't able to work independently.

We really liked what one trainer would say. They would tell the new employees, "One week from now, I'm not going to be here to answer your questions. I want you to be able to succeed in that moment. So let's see if you can find the answer on your own. Then in one week, when you aren't sure what to do, you will know that you can find the guidance you need, even when I'm not around."

That is a trainer that is seeking to empower their employees instead of just being the "sage on the stage."

Another common problem is a trainer who is communicating actionable knowledge verbally to fill in knowledge gaps. Jonathan, our implementation specialist at ScreenSteps, would often sit in on training sessions and hear trainers start adding additional information to the guides. He would ask, "Is the information you are sharing right now in the guides? Why not?"

The guides were quickly updated because if they weren't, then the organization would just be forced back into relying on tribal knowledge again. The digital guides should be able to stand alone.

If trainers are filling in a lot of foundational knowledge gaps, then you should modify your foundational training materials to include that information. If trainers are filling in a lot of actionable knowledge gaps, then you absolutely need to improve the guides.

Misconceptions, Mistakes, and Surprises

Trainers who are new to the Find & Follow Framework often carry some misconceptions, make some common mistakes, and experience several surprises during the training sessions.

Misconceptions

There are four common misconceptions:

1. "If I don't say it, they won't learn it."
2. The digital guides are just training wheels.
3. Memorization is necessary.
4. Quizzes are required.

If I don't say it, they won't learn it.

How can employees learn information if we don't tell it to them? That is a significant concern that most trainers have.

As a trainer, you need to trust that the learning will happen as the employees go through the practice activities. You will find that in a Find & Follow Training, they will learn much more than you ever actually verbalize.

The digital guides are just training wheels.

The digital guides are *not* the backup plan, and they are not training wheels. They are *the* plan. They are the bike employees who are going to ride every day to arrive at their destination.

Memorization is necessary.

This one goes along with the belief that the guides are just training wheels. It does not matter if an employee can recite a process back to you from memory. They are going to rely on a perfectly accurate and consistent digital guide instead of their imperfect memories. All that matters is that they can find it and follow it.

Quizzes are required.
Because memorization is not required, neither are quizzes. The test is whether or not the employee can complete the activity successfully, not whether they can answer an arbitrary set of questions in a quiz or test. Performance is the proof of their competency, not a 10-question quiz.

Mistakes

Here are some common mistakes:

1. Trying to crush employees on the first exercise
2. Jumping in to help too soon
3. Demanding perfection the first time through

Trying to Crush Employees on the First Exercise
We mentioned this above, but it bears repeating. All too often, we see trainers that want to start with the most difficult and convoluted process the employee could ever encounter. It's the equivalent of taking a high school baseball player and asking him to hit against a major league pitcher for his first at-bat. It's not going to lead to success.

Start slow. Give them some softballs. Help them build confidence. You will be amazed at how quickly they progress.

Jumping in to Help Too Soon
Then there is the opposite end of the spectrum. There are trainers who hate to see people struggle, so they jump in to offer assistance anytime the employee gets stuck. We once had a trainer say that they didn't want anyone to feel uncomfortable during training.

Learning and gaining independence is often uncomfortable. If you try to avoid making your employees uncomfortable during training, then you are ensuring that they will be helpless after training.

Let employees struggle a bit. As they work to figure things out, they will learn more than you could ever teach them by jumping in every time they get stuck.

Yes, there will be times when you need to offer assistance or provide additional clarification. There may be times when you need to redesign a guide that just isn't clear. But give the employee a bit of time to work through the problem before you try to help them.

Demanding Perfection the First Time Through

Some trainers think the digital guides aren't working when employees don't perform perfectly the first time. Apparently, they never crashed their bike while trying to learn to ride it.

The employees are learning how to follow digital guides. For many, that will be a new skill. A few stumbles are to be expected. But you should quickly see by the fourth or fifth run-through that the employee's confidence is increasing. Give them the space to stumble until they can run.

Surprises

After they complete their first Find & Follow Training event, many trainers are surprised by what they experience.

1. Employees don't naturally know how to read and follow directions.
2. Their guides aren't as complete or easy to follow as they thought.
3. Employees learn so much more than what they were taught.

Employees don't naturally know how to read and follow directions.

Trainers are surprised at how bad most employees are at reading and following instructions. Our team has run trainings where employees kept making mistakes because they simply wouldn't read what was on the screen. The trainer had to keep encouraging the employee to trust the guide.

Following digital guides is a learned skill. It doesn't take long to learn, but it needs to be learned. It won't come naturally to everyone.

Their guides aren't as complete or easy to follow as they thought.

It is disappointing when someone struggles to follow a guide you created that you were sure was crystal clear. It is completely normal to have to adjust and improve the guides during training. Just accept that it won't be perfect the first time and iterate quickly until the guides are working effectively.

Employees learn so much more than what they were taught.

Trainers are astonished at how much information the employees learn that the trainer never taught them. Those digital guides are full of information about your policies and procedures. As they go through the practice exercises, new hires will have many ah-ha moments when concepts and procedures will just click. And because they will discover these concepts, policies, and procedures on their own, it will stick with them much longer than if a trainer had recited the information while showing a slide deck.

Dealing With Challenges and Objections

Challenge: Processes Are Too Complicated

This is the biggest objection we hear. "Our processes are just too complicated." There may be situations where this is true, but we have dealt with some pretty complex industries—medical device manufacturers, public utilities with multiple backend systems, medical scheduling, software as a service, transportation, retail, health insurance, telecommunications, IT support shops, and financial service companies. Each of these groups has had to deal with its own form of complexity.

Solution: Clarify the Process

In most cases, processes are more unclear than complicated. When something isn't clear, it can seem very, very complicated. My wife makes fantastic potato salad. When I would try to make it, I would ask how much of this or that ingredient I should put in. She would reply, "I don't know. I just put in the amount that looks about right."

Not helpful at all. That lack of clarity makes the process of making potato salad seem complex. But when we get some clarity about how much of each ingredient to add, what was once complex all of a sudden becomes simple. I'm not going to lie; adding clarity to some processes can be tricky and takes some practice. But it can be done. See the chapter "Building Digital Guides That Can Stand Alone" for suggestions on how to achieve this.

When somebody says that a process is complex, what that usually means is that they don't really know how they do something. They just go off their gut and don't have a process. That doesn't mean that the process can't be documented—it just means that they haven't done the work of figuring out the "recipe." Any process can be improved with digital guides, even if that process is extremely complex.

Challenge: No One Has Time to Create or Maintain the Digital Guides

This is really two concerns that get conflated into one.

1. We don't have enough time to create the initial guides we would need in place to launch a Find & Follow program.
2. We don't have time to maintain those digital guides after we launch a Find & Follow program.

Challenge: Maintaining the Guides

These are real and valid concerns, but let's deal with the last one first. When a supervisor says this, based on their current situation, they are right. If they had to keep doing all the things they are doing today (fixing mistakes, answering questions, filling in gaps for employees who don't know what to do), then they would be correct. They won't have enough time.

Solution: Focus on the Future State

But that isn't how life is like in a Find & Follow Organization. After Find & Follow is launched, those supervisors have increased bandwidth. The change is dramatic.

You need to realize that once your Find & Follow program is running, your supervisors are going to spend much less time answering questions and fixing problems. Part of that increased bandwidth can be directed toward maintaining the guides. It takes much less time to answer a question once than it does to answer it a dozen times.

One of our clients "flipped the script" on their supervisors. They explained that they wanted them to invest their time in preventing problems as opposed to responding to problems after they happened.

It turned out that fixing problems took a lot more time than preventing them.

Once they made that shift, Tier 1 agents began asking what the supervisors and senior agents were going to do now that the Tier 1 agents weren't escalating calls to them anymore.

In another contact center, the supervisor only has to get involved in situations that are new or where a process hasn't been established. Otherwise, everything is documented. She has time to create digital guides because she isn't bothered by more routine questions.

Updating a guide is an investment. It means you answer a question once instead of answering it 100 times. It means you solve a problem before you have to fix a mistake.

So, maintaining the guides is not a problem. But getting the initial batch of guides created can be a daunting task.

Challenge: Creating the Initial Batch of Guides

This is more of a challenge. Depending on the complexity of the business, there can be a substantial effort involved in creating enough digital guides to really make an impact on operations.

We have found that it is helpful to reframe the problem. Instead of thinking, "How am I going to find time to get all of these created?" ask yourself, "How few guides could I create before I would save my team enough time that we would have the bandwidth to work on the rest of the guides?"

Solution: The 80% Launch

Not all guides are created equal. Some guides will save an employee five minutes once a month. Some will save them 20 minutes every week. Some will save them an hour a day. Review the chapter titled "Doing an 80% Launch" and apply those principles.

If 80% seems like too much to do, then start with the ten guides that would make the biggest impact. In the vast majority of cases, it is just a few unclear and complex processes that cause the majority of the problems.

We had one client that just focused on the top 15–20 transaction types that their team was responsible for handling. With less than 20 guides, they saw a major impact on their operations.

If you think of your team's time as having a monetary value, you can start seeing your efforts as either investments or expenses. Answering a question using tribal knowledge is a payment, just like spending your time creating a digital guide is a payment. But creating a digital guide is also an investment that will create more free time in the future.

Make sure your initial investments are in digital guides that will produce a large return in saved time, and you will quickly free up the bandwidth to complete all your remaining guides.

Solution: Jump-Starting the Launch

Another option is to have a team come in and jump-start the process for you. If they are trained in the Find & Follow Framework, they will be able to help you do the following:

- Run the Find & Follow Workshop and identify the most impactful guides.
- Review your existing documentation and resources to determine what content can be used as is or at least as a starting point.
- Create the initial 80% of guides and submit them for review and feedback from your team.

Your team just has to approve the guides instead of creating them from scratch. This allows for a much faster launch with less impact on your team's bandwidth.

If this is something you need help with, reach out to our team. We are happy to help.

Scan this QR code to get in touch with the authors of this book.

www.screensteps.com/find-follow-book/contact-us

Challenge: Employees Won't Use the Guides

A lot of people say, "Nobody will use the guides." And for many, that has been their actual experience in past knowledge management projects. But that is a little like having an empty restaurant full of food that no one wants to eat and claiming that the low sales are due to a bad location.

The problem isn't that employees hate knowledge bases. If that were true, Google wouldn't get 8.5 billion searches per day. It's that employees don't like to work too hard for answers. If they search a knowledge base and get a document that is 50 pages long and written by an engineer or a lawyer, they're going to close it and simply ask "Steve" what to do.

When you apply the Find & Follow principles, your digital guides are simple to find and easy to follow. Employees like that.

One of our clients had almost 790,000 digital guide views in their first year of using Find & Follow with only 700 employees. That was an average of about 100 guide views per month per employee.

Here are some approaches that we have found really drive adoption of the digital guides.

Solution: Incorporate Digital Guides Into New Hire Training

Sometimes we will see organizations create Find & Follow guides but never train their employees to follow them. Employees are going to do what you train them to do. If they learn to ask the instructor or supervisor for help during your new hire training, then that is what they are going to do once they leave training. But if they are taught to find and follow digital guides, then that is what they will do when they are working independently.

The fact is, many people are not good at following instructions because they don't trust the instructions. In the past, instructions have been hard to follow, inaccurate, or incomplete, so people are used to skimming documentation and then either winging it or asking for help.

But with the right design and just a little training and a little practice, employees can develop the simple skills needed to find and follow your digital guides. It is like learning to use a GPS. At first, it was an unfamiliar experience, and you may have even doubted what it was telling you (resulting in lots of U-turns). But after a little practice, you can follow the GPS and go anywhere you want.

Solution: Never Answer a Question That Is Already in the Guides

If employees ask you a question, you need to point them back to the digital guides. If you answer the question when the answer already exists in the digital guides, then you are re-enforcing bad habits.

One approach that can be effective is to say, "Let's see if we have a guide for that. Have you already tried to find one?"

If they have and can't find one, take a moment and create it. If they haven't looked yet, encourage them to try to find one. This doesn't have to be done in an accusatory or demeaning way. Just reinforce that you are trying to make sure that they have the resources they need to work independently, and the digital guides are the key to making that happen.

Solution: Hold Employees, and Your Guides, Accountable

Accountability is important in a Find & Follow Organization — accountability for the employees, the digital guides, and the people that create those guides.

If a mistake is made in a process, the first step is to see if the employee followed the digital guide. If they didn't, then they need to take responsibility for attempting to work from memory and not using the tools that have been designed to help them be knowledgeable, consistent, and efficient in their work.

If they *did* use the guide and still made a mistake, then the guide needs to be held responsible. Look at the guide and try to understand why it was misunderstood or misapplied. Are there changes you could make that would prevent the same error from happening? Don't blame employees if the guide isn't clear. Accept responsibility for making it "dummy proof" and improve it.

Those in charge of maintaining the guides need to take responsibility for making updates right away when necessary. Remember that your employees are relying on these guides to do their jobs. They can't afford to wait around for a week to have an important update made to one of the guides they use.

That is one of the reasons that it is so important that you settle on a knowledge operations tool that allows for rapid updates to content.

Creating Clarity When Procedures Seem Complicated

As we mentioned previously, one of the biggest challenges can be creating guides for very complex processes. It is certainly a skill that needs to be learned. The good news is that with practice, you and your team will become more and more confident in helping employees navigate complex procedures.

The first step is to not declare defeat before you even start. While it can seem overwhelming at first, we have never encountered a process that couldn't be clarified with some careful analysis and brainstorming. Embrace the fact that you won't design it perfectly the first time but that with some determination and iteration, you will quickly get to an ideal flow.

Tips before your start:
1. This won't be perfect the first time. This is going to be an iterative process.
2. You always want to talk to the person who is actually doing the work (not their manager).
3. Be inquisitive. Make them explain it to you as if you were a five-year-old.

Follow these steps to document the process:

1. Write down the question.
2. Create the critical path.
3. Fill in the branches.
4. Test, iterate, and optimize.
5. Don't overstuff the guide.

Write Down the Question You Need to Answer

We talked about this in the section on making your digital guides findable, but it is just as important when trying to document a complex process. By getting the title right, you will be setting the boundaries around your digital guide.

A title like "How to Work With Accounts" has no boundaries. It is almost impossible to create something that is followable.

But a title like "How to Create a New Account for an LLC" sets some very clear boundaries for the content of the digital guide.

Make sure that your title helps you clearly identify the question you need to answer in the digital guide.

Use Their Language

Another tip on titles: Use the language your employees use. Understanding their lingo and putting that lingo into the article titles makes it much easier for employees to find and understand the digital guides.

Talk Them Through The Process: Create the Critical Path

Now pretend you are talking someone through this process on the phone. We like to call these "Conversation Flows" because they should follow the form of a conversation. Here is an example between a supervisor (S) and employee (E):

E: How do I create a new invoice for this customer?

S: What type of customer is it, a business or individual?

E: A business.

S: OK, first, you need to create a company record. Go to the "Companies" tab in the CRM.

S: Then click New Company.

S: Do you already have their billing address?

E: No.

S: Reach out to the customer and request their billing address.

Etc.

Just follow this all the way through to its completion. For every question where there are multiple answers or branches in the process, make a note of the branch and move on. You don't need to fill them out yet.

You can either jot this down in a bulleted list format (making sub-bullets for branches), or you can use a visual diagramming tool like Miro, Visio, or Lucidchart. These tools are very helpful for defining the flow of a process.

Fill in the Branches

Once you have completed the critical path, go back, and follow the path for each alternate branch in the process. As you proceed, don't worry about repeating yourself. Just get things down as best you can, even if you are repeating certain sections.

Test, Iterate, and Optimize

Finally, take the flow and start testing it on real-world scenarios. Iterate quickly, and find places to optimize. You will probably discover new variables that you hadn't considered. That is fine. Incorporate them in. Remember that the goal is not to have a perfectly optimized decision tree. The goal is to have a decision tree that will navigate an employee through the process correctly every time. Focus on clarity first and optimization later.

Don't Overstuff the Guide

When people first start creating guides for complex processes, there is a temptation to overstuff the guide by creating one master guide for every possible situation. For example, contact centers will often want to make one guide that handles every possible call the agent might receive. This results in a decision tree that is massive, hard to navigate, and impossible to maintain.

A better strategy is to have a separate guide for each specific procedure. You can train your employees to find the right guide when they need it or even link to guides from other guides. But don't create one massive guide. You and your employees will regret the inflexibility it will create when changes happen.

Tips

Here are a few helpful guidelines:

- Experiment with reordering the sequence of your questions. You may find that you can dramatically shorten the process by shifting the order of the questions.
- Try to short-circuit the process as quickly as possible. If there is a path that would cause an employee to have to end the process right away, move the question that would identify that path up as early as possible in the guide. That will save everyone time when that scenario occurs.
- Think of designing this process as a rough sketch that will eventually become a detailed drawing. You aren't going to complete things in the first pass. As you pass over it multiple times, you will start to fill in all the blank spots and create a complete picture.

Using this approach and these tips, you will be able to tackle even your most complex procedures.

Choosing a Knowledge Base or Knowledge Ops Platform

Hopefully, by now, you realize that you can't really run a Find & Follow program on Word, PDF, PowerPoint, and SharePoint. You, at the very least, need a modern knowledge base platform and, ideally, a knowledge ops platform.

A knowledge ops platform is like a knowledge base but better. The problem with most knowledge bases is that they lack the tools necessary to build digital guides that are followable and scannable.

Basic Requirements for a Knowledge Base Platform

Whatever software you choose, here is what it will need to be able to do:

- Build standard articles, interactive checklists, and decision trees
- Gather analytics around usage and search requests
- Allow users to comment on and give feedback on the digital guides

Without these basic capabilities, it will be difficult for your team to design digital guides that are up to date.

Additional Benefits of a Knowledge Ops Platform

A knowledge ops platform is going to have additional tools to help you operationalize your knowledge, ensure that it stays up to date, and ensure your employees use the digital guides regularly.

A knowledge ops platform will have capabilities around the following areas:

- All the functionality of a knowledge base
- Integrated courses for presenting foundational knowledge
- Authoring and updating tools that allow for very rapid content creation and iteration
- Tools and integration to allow employees to access the digital guides in the applications they commonly use as well as on mobile or tablet devices
- Tools for notifying employees of changes to the digital guides

At our company, we sell a knowledge ops platform called ScreenSteps. Its tools have been specifically designed to support the Find & Follow Framework, and it is the platform our clients used to achieve all the client outcomes mentioned in this book.

You can learn more at www.screensteps.com.

Using a Knowledge Ops Platform to Implement the Four Systems of Find & Follow

A knowledge ops platform will help you in each of the Find & Follow systems (Prepare, Train, Empower, and Adapt).

Prepare

A knowledge ops platform will primarily help you in the Design + Refine stages of the Prepare System. The goals of the Design + Refine stage are:

1. To create digital guides that are findable, followable, and scannable
2. Iterate quickly on those guides until employees can use them without supervisor assistance

With a knowledge ops platform, you will:

- Have the tools you need to create decision trees, add screenshots and images, add interactive checklists, and make key information stand out with styled text blocks
- Create and update content quickly

It is not only crucial that you can add the interactive elements such as decision trees and collapsible sections to your digital guides—you have to be able to do it quickly without requiring any coding.

We sometimes see customers trying to accomplish this functionality in a knowledge base by adding custom HTML, Javascript, and CSS. The problem is it just takes too long, so you can't achieve the second goal—rapid iteration.

Rapid iteration is key to success. With a knowledge ops platform, you will be able to iterate more quickly.

Train

A part of the Train System is incorporating foundational courses. A knowledge ops platform will allow you to create foundational courses that are integrated with the digital guides.

This makes it very easy to link to or reference digital guides in your courses and prevents your authoring team from having to maintain content in both an LMS and your knowledge base.

Empower

With a knowledge ops platform, your supervisors will be able to:

- Hold employees accountable for using the digital guides by reviewing usage reports
- Quickly create new digital guides when employees encounter questions or tasks that haven't been addressed
- Analyze search reports to identify knowledge gaps in the platform and then add additional guides

Your employees will be able to:

- Add feedback to articles
- Request new articles when they can't find what they need

Adapt

As we have already stated, a knowledge operations platform will help you quickly update content when things change. One of the key tools is the ability to rapidly replace screenshots. Replacing screenshots can take hours and hours with traditional knowledge bases, making major changes extremely difficult.

A knowledge operations platform will also allow you to notify your employees of important changes in procedures and even require that they acknowledge the notification.

The ability to notify employees of changes will dramatically decrease the need for repeat training sessions.

You can learn more about all these capabilities and others at www.screensteps.com.

The Short Version of Everything

Why: You will improve every aspect of your business if you can transfer knowledge to your employees more quickly.

How: The Find & Follow Framework will help you stop relying on tribal knowledge and memorization and allow you to transfer knowledge almost instantly to your employees.

What Will This Impact?

- Training time
- Onboarding time
- Task time
- Error rates
- Change readiness
- Stress levels
- Confidence

What Is the Framework?

The framework consists of four systems to help you transfer knowledge:

1. Prepare
2. Train
3. Empower
4. Adapt

Prepare

- Align + Define
    - Run a Find & Follow Workshop to align your training and operations teams and define exactly what your employees need to be able to do.
- Design + Refine
    - Separate foundational and actionable knowledge.
    - Design digital guides that an employee can find and follow without the assistance of a supervisor.
    - Refine them until they meet your performance needs.

Train

- Break out your topics.
- Prepare foundational courses.
- Prepare practice activities.
- Run the training sessions.
    - For each topic, do the following:
        - Present the foundational course.
        - Introduce the guides.
        - Run the practice activities.

Empower

- Rely on the digital guides.
- Redirect questions back to the digital guides.
- If there are gaps, invest in updating guides or creating new ones instead of relying on tribal knowledge.

Adapt

- Analyze the impact of the change.
- Prepare the digital guides.
- Train or notify.

Who Does This?

Your knowledge ops team.

- The knowledge ops team will, at a minimum, include a supervisor, trainer, and an experienced employee in the target role.
- Each team should designate a Knowledge Champion.
- The Knowledge Champion runs the workshops, creates and maintains the guides, identifies gaps, and fills them.
- Larger organizations may want to use a Knowledge Ops Manager to train and support multiple Knowledge Champions in the organization.

What Tech Do I Need?

Knowledge base software that can support standard articles, interactive checklists, and interactive decision trees. An even better solution is a knowledge ops platform. Learn more at www.screensteps.com.

How Long Does It Take to Implement?

From two weeks to six months, depending on the complexity of the environment and the resources you dedicate to it. Typically, it takes between 6–12 weeks.

Is It Worth It?

Yes! You will never want to go back to relying on tribal knowledge after you have experienced what it is like to work in a Find & Follow Organization.

Additional Online Resources and Training

If you prefer to learn in a course format, you can access accompanying courses at:
www.screensteps.com/find-follow-book/courses

Download a FREE Find & Follow workbook:
www.screensteps.com/find-follow-book/workbook

Download PDF versions of the Knowledge Ops Maturity Model and the Knowledge Ops flywheel, as well as additional resources at:
www.screensteps.com/find-follow-book/resources

ScreenSteps offers Find & Follow training to organizations of all sizes. To learn more, visit www.screensteps.com/find-follow-book/training.

Acknowledgments

It turns out that writing a book is a lot harder than it sounds. While Jonathan and Greg are ultimately responsible for anything good or bad that is written on these pages, this book couldn't have come about without the help of many people.

We need to thank our marketing team at ScreenSteps: Rebecca Lane, John Julien, and Brittany Oehlhof. They have spent countless hours helping us refine terminology, clarify examples, and remove unnecessary detail. We are blessed to work with each of them.

Our brother and co-founder, Trevor DeVore, has also been a key contributor. Trevor and Greg co-founded Blue Mango Multimedia (which later became ScreenSteps) back in 2003. There was no master plan, just a series of events that brought some opportunities together. Without Trevor's technical expertise and the tools he has provided us, we never would have been able to explore the concepts behind Find & Follow.

Feedback from another brother, Nathan DeVore, was also extremely helpful.

Editing and proofreading was performed by Sky Rodio Nuttall, Rebecca Lane, and Dorothy DeVore. Thank you for smoothing out the rough edges in our writing!

The concepts in this book and in the Find & Follow Framework have been heavily influenced by several other authors and thought leaders, including Atul Gawande, Greg McKeown, Clayton Christensen, Cathy Moore, Julie Dirksen, Dr. Conrad Gottfredson, Bob Mosher, and Stephen Covey.

Our parents have always believed we could do anything, despite all evidence to the contrary. They have been supportive at every stage of our lives. We are so blessed to have been born into their family.

Greg would like to thank his wife, Holly. She certainly didn't know what she was in for when they were married 28 years ago. She is his true partner, his best friend, and dedicated supporter through all the challenges they have faced together.

Jonathan would like to thank his wife, Laura, for being such a strong support to him and their four children and for always giving Jonathan a space to explore new ideas and talk through the challenges that he faces at work and in life. Love you!

Finally, we want to acknowledge the Lord's influence in our lives. We don't believe in coincidences. We really do believe that everything happens for a reason. As we look back on our personal lives and the events of our business over the last 20 years, we can see His hand in so many ways.

The insight that came when the challenge seemed unsolvable.

The customer who would be willing to perform a bold experiment right when we needed a break.

The gift of hope when hope seemed to be so hard to find.

Acknowledgments

The path has been anything but straight, but looking back, we can see His hand at every turn and His footsteps beside us during every long march.

Greg and Jonathan DeVore – July 2023

About the Authors

Greg DeVore is the co-founder and CEO of ScreenSteps, a company dedicated to helping organizations transfer knowledge to their employees more efficiently.

His career in training began 20 years ago in the film scoring industry, where he taught composers to utilize Apple's Logic platform. This experience paved the way for opportunities to design e-learning solutions for medical devices for prominent companies such as GE, Siemens, and Philips.

As the CEO of ScreenSteps, Greg collaborates with organizations of various sizes to replace ineffective training programs with efficient knowledge transfer strategies, enabling them to onboard employees at least 50% faster.

Greg holds a degree in Composition and Film Scoring from the Berklee College of Music. He resides in McLean, Virginia, with his wife and four boys, which explains the abundance of broken items in their home.

Jonathan DeVore is the lead consultant at ScreenSteps helping organizations of all sizes implement the Find & Follow Framework.

Jonathan's career began as a CPA at PwC, where he assisted federal clients in improving their information security policies.

He identified that effective knowledge transfer was a persistent challenge in environments where compliance was crucial, and change was a constant factor.

Later, Jonathan joined his two brothers at ScreenSteps to continue innovating knowledge transfer strategies and tactics. Over the past decade, he has worked hands-on with clients to determine what works in theory and what actually works in practice.

Jonathan is a professional jack-of-all-trades, which has honed his problem-solving skills. He holds a bachelor's degree in accounting and a master's degree in clinical mental health counseling. He enjoys performing magic and playing the piano for any willing audience.

He resides in Huntersville, North Carolina, with his wife and four children.

About ScreenSteps

ScreenSteps is a knowledge operations solution that helps organizations overcome employee training and performance challenges by solving their root problem—an inability to transfer knowledge efficiently from those who know to those who do.

Our knowledge operations solution tackles knowledge transfer problems by providing you with two things:
- Software tools for creating digital guides and courses and hosting them in an online knowledge base
- Consulting Services to help organizations implement the Find & Follow Framework, making knowledge transfer more effective

To learn more about our products and services, please email us at book@screensteps.com or go to www.screensteps.com/book.

Made in the USA
Middletown, DE
18 June 2025